The
SOCCER MOMS'
COOKBOOK

The
SOCCER MOMS'
COOKBOOK

Healthy meals and snacks for active kids

CARLA OVERBECK

**Former captain of the Olympic and World Cup
Champion Women's U.S. Soccer Team**

WITH PAM MASTERS, R.D.

Acknowledgment

We'd like to thank American Youth Soccer Organization (AYSO) for their assistance with many of the photographs in this book and for helping to put this book together.

AYSO is committed to the physical and mental development of all children and develops and delivers quality youth soccer programs nationwide.

AYSO soccer programs are based on philosophies and principles that promote a fun, family environment, encourage respect and fair play, and ensure that "everyone plays."

If you would like more information about AYSO, please visit http://soccer.org or call:1-800-USA-AYSO.

Text and Recipes: Carla Overbeck and Pam Masters, R.D.

Project Editor: Lisa M. Tooker

Editor: Howard Cohl

Copy Editor: Ann Beman

Design and Layout: Elizabeth Watson

Photography: **AYSO:** soccer ball, back cover, 21 (left), 22, 23, 24, 28, 29, 30, 33, 34, 45, 46–47, 50, 51, 52–53, 54–55, 56, 68, 80, 85, 86–87, 89, 102, 104–105, 112, 113, 122–123, 124, 125, 128, 129, 135, 137, 143, 146, 147; **Perry McIntyre, Jr. (all rights reserved:** 9, 10, 12, 15, 72-73; **Carla Overbeck:** front flap, 6, 8, 13, 14; **PictureArts:** 6, 16, 17, 21 (right), 25, 26, 27, 35, 37, 38, 39, 43, 44, 48, 58–59, 60–61, 62–63, 64, 65, 70, 71, 74, 75, 76–77, 78, 79, 82–83, 92–93, 94, 95, 99, 100, 106, 110, 111, 114–115, 116, 118, 127, 132–133, 138–139, 141; Cover image, 3: **Copyright 2005 Treleven Photography, Inc.**

Printed in China

ISBN 1-59637-043-2

To my family.

—Carla Overbeck

To great family and friends.

—Pam Masters

 # Introduction

The crowning achievement for women's soccer occurred on July 10, 1999, in Pasadena, California. The United States played The People's Republic of China in front of a worldwide television audience of 1 billion, plus 90,000 screaming fans at the Rose Bowl. It seemed the entire country had rallied behind the team, and the players were riding an unexpected groundswell of support from the media and the general public. As President Clinton later said, the game "brought America to its feet, had us screaming our lungs out with pride and joy." The two teams played 90 minutes to a scoreless tie, and after two overtime periods, faced a penalty kick shootout to determine the World Cup champion. It was a tension-filled climax to the biggest event in the history of women's team sports.

I was the captain of the U.S. team. This was the pinnacle of my sports dreams—and a huge responsibility. Not only did I have to play well myself, I needed to inspire my teammates to play their best, too. Fortunately, this team needed little motivation. We were a group of dedicated athletes who had developed an undeniable will. Every player, every game, left her heart on the field. We also had the advantage of knowing we were the fittest team in the tournament.

From the beginning, the U.S. women's soccer team had faced an uphill battle to establish itself on the world stage. We had not grown up in a culture of soccer like the women we faced from Brazil, Germany, China, and Norway. Our role models tended to be football, basketball, and baseball players, and we had not developed soccer skills from infancy.

Still, we knew we were athletic enough and fit enough to play anyone. We had sworn we would never be outworked, and that no team would ever beat us because they were in better shape.

How did we become a team so confident in its fitness level? What training regimen did we follow? As you would expect, we spent hours working out, lifting weights, and practicing. We also had the help of the best trainers, masseuses, and physical therapists in the world. Just as importantly, we had

the services of world-class nutritionists who helped us determine the best diet we could follow to realize our maximum potential.

We had learned the importance of good nutrition in the early days of the U.S. National team. We had taken several trips to China to play in international tournaments and had noticed a dramatic drop in energy and fitness levels in our times there. During one three-week event, I lost almost 10 pounds; and I didn't need to lose an ounce! We were unaccustomed to the food we were being served, and most of us existed on a diet of hot chocolate, cereal, and instant oatmeal we kept in our hotel rooms. By the final game I was weak. I had neglected to meet my basic nutritional needs.

By 1991, when China hosted the inaugural women's World Cup, we had learned our lesson. We brought our own chefs with us (in fact, I ended up marrying one of them!). We feasted on pasta, veggies, marinara sauce, and other healthy foods we were used to eating back home. We maintained our energy level, stayed fit, and won the final over a tough, resilient Norwegian team. After that experience, our team was in tune with proper nutrition. Leading up to the Olympic Games we won in 1996 and that unforgettable World Cup in 1999, we depended on the best nutritionists to help us attain our peak performance. We realized nutrition could be the difference between winning and losing. Fortunately, our hard work and perseverance paid off, and we were very successful. I'm also proud to say we kept our promise—we were always the fittest team on the field!

Today, I enjoy a new sort of pride. My eight-year-old son, Jackson, is now involved in all sorts of sports himself. He's terrific, although soccer is not his main love. And my two-year-old daughter, Carson, is starting to kick a ball around. Surprisingly enough, I'm now a bona fide soccer mom!

When Jackson first started attending school, I immediately noticed that many of the other kids were overweight. That's not surprising, I suppose, since excess weight has become a growing national epidemic in children. I think we should consider it a national disgrace. It's bad enough when adults overeat and become fat. But there is no reason kids should be allowed to become so out of shape. How could well-meaning and otherwise responsible parents neglect exercise and allow "bad for you" eating?

As I watched the snacks many of the kids brought to the soccer games—and when I listened to them tell me how they were all planning to go get burgers or a giant pizza after the game—I started to understand. Getting in shape and staying in shape begins with eating the right food. It has to be nutritionally balanced, give us the right mix of muscle-building and energy-producing calories, keep us at (or, in some cases bring us down to) the right weight, and taste good.

No one can play competitive sports successfully if they regularly snack on candy bars and potato chips or habitually eat double-cheese burgers. On the other hand, no one wants to live exclusively on carrot sticks and sugar-free granola. I eat healthy foods most of the time, but I love candy. Would I be better off if I never touched it? Of course, but an occasional slip of "bad for you" food won't hurt you—as long as it is occasional. The trick, of course, is to get kids to enjoy and hopefully crave nutritionally sound foods. What's the only way to establish a diet that complements an athletic lifestyle? Find nutritionally balanced dishes that taste great. One without the other just won't work.

Of course, that's easy to say and hard to do. In all the hustle and bustle involved in working, raising children, maintaining a household, trying to stay in shape ourselves, and living some semblance of a well-rounded life;

good, nutritious food often gets lost in the shuffle. It's so much easier to pop into a fast food restaurant on the way home from work (or after soccer practice) and pick up some fried chicken, burgers, or a milkshake. That sort of food tastes good, too. Fast food chains spend millions of dollars on market research to figure out what foods, regardless of their nutritional values, appeal to our over-stimulated palates. But it's not good for the kids, and it's not good for you either.

So what's the solution?

What moms need, I realized, is a cookbook that does a lot of the work for us. What we need, is a book that provides simple, tasty meals and snacks that are nutritionally balanced for the young athlete, and quick and easy to prepare.

With the help of my friend and registered dietitian Pam Masters, that's what this book is all about. Every meal is nutritionally balanced and healthy, and contains the right mix of vitamins and minerals. No recipe will take you more than a short while to prepare (not counting time when you're not involved, such as marinating time). And, we trust, you'll discover that they taste great!

I hope you'll enjoy it and start on the road to proper nutrition and fitness. An ongoing commitment to exercise and sensible eating is the only diet truly guaranteed to get you and your children fit for life. I hope this cookbook can help you and your kids start realizing the joys of a fit lifestyle.

1 Foundations of Nutrition for Active Kids

Soccer moms *n*. Defined in a number of different ways, we're career women and "domestic goddesses." We have school-age children whom we chauffeur to and from school, various athletic events, and friends. We coach, we cheer, and, most importantly, we strive to find a proper balance between work and family. Maybe we're even the captain of the U.S. women's soccer team! Regardless, we love and care for our families and try to do our best to feed and nurture them. With the statistics of the day revealing increases in childhood obesity, are we failing? No. We're simply challenged by the ongoing busyness of each day, and we're bombarded with the latest food, nutrition, and fitness tips that often seem to create more chaos than assurance.

Food is supposed to be nourishing, energizing, and pleasurable. Food contributes a wide array of textures, tastes, and nutrients, such as carbohydrate, fat, protein, vitamins, minerals, and even water. The first three nutrients listed—carbohydrate, fat, and protein—are known as types of macronutrients. One of their major functions is to provide calories.

Carbohydrate and protein contribute four calories per gram, whereas fat contributes nine calories per gram. Fat obviously provides more calorie density than the other two nutrients, which is one of the reasons why fat intake should be low to moderate, and portions should be controlled to complement foods, rather than overpower them.

Vitamins and minerals are important micronutrients found in a wide variety of foods. Each food item contributes a varying amount, so it is important to vary selections to help meet the body's nutrient needs.

Water is a vital nutrient for the body, as it is a part of every cell and tissue. Besides helping regulate body temperature, water carries nutrients to cells and removes waste products.

So in looking at these six key nutrients, how can we make sure we consume a variety to meet optimal nutrition needs? For quite some time, we used the Basic Four Food Groups as our foundation. However, research has continued to prove that the nutrients found in many fruits and vegetables

play such strong roles in disease prevention that the two were separated. Thus the birth of the Food Guide Pyramid in 1992, which has served as a visual tool to identify the different food groups and the nutrients they represent, as well as provide education on standard portion sizes. As a result of the updated Dietary Guidelines in January 2005, the U.S. Department of Agriculture (USDA) released a new food guidance system in April 2005: *MyPyramid*. The new system intends to complement the 2005 Dietary Guidelines as well as allow more personalization and encouragement for physical activity, amongst other things. The website MyPyramid.gov has even been established to allow for interactive nutrition education. Regardless of the tool used, the message remains the same and is emphasized in the updated Dietary Guidelines of 2005: healthy eating emphasizes fruits, vegetables, whole grains, reduced-fat dairy products, and a variety of lean meats, poultry, fish, beans, eggs, and nuts.

How does this basic nutrition foundation compare to the needs of the athlete? It whole-heartedly supports it! This means the daily recommendations for promoting good health are basically the same for physically active kids, and if anything, provide even more support for consuming plenty of carbohydrates, such as vegetables, fruits, and whole grains. This is especially true in highly aerobic sports such as soccer. Just as a car needs fuel to function, carbohydrates are the body's primary fueling source during exercise. The body stores carbohydrate as glycogen in muscles (kind of like fuel tanks). Too little glycogen can cause fatigue and decrease performance mentally and physically; consistent intake, with replenishment after training and games, is ideal.

Nutrition Goals for Balanced Eating

Daily calorie intake distribution for all:	Daily calorie intake distribution specific to athletes:
45–65 percent carbohydrate	55–75 percent carbohydrate
25–35 percent fat	25–30 percent fat
10–35 percent protein	15–20 percent protein

Child-Specific 2005 Dietary Guidelines

Dietary Guideline Key Recommendations for Children and Adolescents

Adequate Nutrients within Calorie Needs

- Consume a variety of nutrient-dense foods and beverages within and among the basic food groups, while choosing foods that limit the intake of saturated and *trans* fats, cholesterol, added sugars, and salt.

Weight Management

- Overweight children–reduce the rate of body weight gain, while allowing growth and development. Consult a healthcare provider before placing a child on a weight-reduction diet.

Physical Activity

- Engage in at least 60 minutes of physical activity on most, preferably all, days of the week to promote health, psychological well-being, and a healthy body weight.

Food Groups to Encourage

- Choose a variety of fruits and vegetables each day. In particular, select from all five vegetable subgroups (dark green, orange, legumes, starchy vegetables, and other vegetables) several times a week.
- Consume whole-grain products often; at least half the grains should be whole grains. Children 2 to 8 years of age should consume 2 cups per day of reduced-fat milk or equivalent milk products. Children 9 years of age and older should consume 3 cups per day of reduced-fat milk or equivalent milk products.

Fats

- Keep total fat intake between 30 percent to 35 percent of calories for children 2–3 years of age and between 25–35 percent of calories for children and adolescents 4–8 years of age, with most fats coming from sources of polyunsaturated and monounsaturated fatty acids, such as fish, nuts, and vegetable oils.

Carbohydrates

- Choose fiber-rich fruits, vegetables, and whole grains often.
- Choose and prepare food and beverages with little added sugars or caloric sweeteners.
- Reduce the incidence of dental cavities by practicing good oral hygiene and consuming sugar- and starch-containing foods and beverages less frequently.

Sodium and Potassium

- Consume less than 2300 milligrams of sodium (1 teaspoon salt) per day.
- Choose and prepare foods with little salt. At the same time, consume potassium-rich foods, such as fruits and vegetables.

Alcoholic Beverages

- NOT an option!

Food Safety

- Do not eat or drink raw (unpasteurized) milk or any products made from unpasteurized milk, raw or partially cooked eggs or foods containing raw eggs, raw or undercooked meat and poultry, raw or undercooked fish or shellfish, unpasteurized juices, or raw sprouts.

Providing adequate calories and fluid is also critical for physically active kids. Calorie needs may increase by as much as 800 calories per day depending upon the child's gender, age, and level of activity. We recommend smaller, more frequent feedings rather than one to three large meals per day.

Kids need fluids before, during, and after events. Oftentimes, the body doesn't reliably trigger a desire for fluid intake, so, especially with young athletes, it is important to periodically insist on water breaks. If they're not drinking enough, kids can get dehydrated, which leads to "minor" problems, such as irritability, fatigue, and a sudden decline in performance. Therefore, at all times, be aware of the importance of hydration and the recommendations on consumption, especially for athletes.

In our quest to promote good health, we often give way too much attention to sweets such as soda pop, candy, cookies, and the like, creating issues that may not have otherwise existed. Consuming these in moderation appears to be a more realistic answer than the extremes of total abstinence

Fluid Recommendations for Kids

Daily recommendations:	At least 48 ounces
Two hours prior to the event:	16–20 ounces
During a rigorous event:	4-8 ounces every 15–20 minutes
After the event:	Drink freely; with especially rigorous events, it is advisable to weigh kids prior to the event and immediately following. Replace every pound lost with 16 ounces water.

The source of fluid intake doesn't have to be just water. Many foods, such as watermelon, oranges, and potatoes, have a high fluid content. Be aware of the calorie content of other beverages if they are included, and remember that some may actually intensify thirst rather than replenish it.

Gender-Specific Estimated Calorie Requirements

For Various Age Groups at Three Levels of Physical Activity

Estimated amounts of calories needed to maintain energy balance for various gender and age groups at three different levels of physical activity. The estimates are rounded to the nearest 200 calories and were determined using the Institute of Medicine (IOM) equation.

Gender	Age (years)	Sedentary●●	Moderately Active●●●	Active●●●●
Female	4–8	1200	1400–1600	1400–1800
Female	9–13	1600	1600–2000	1800–2200
Female	14–18	1800	2000	2400
Male	4–8	1400	1400–1600	1600–2000
Male	9–13	1800	1800–2200	2000–2600
Male	14–18	2200	2400–2800	2800–3200

● These levels are based on Estimated Energy Requirements (EER) from the Institute of Medicine Dietary Reference Intakes for macronutrients report, 2002, calculated by gender, age, and activity level for reference-sized individuals. "Reference size," as determined by IOM, is based on median height and weight for ages up to age 18 and median height and weight for that height to give a body mass index (BMI) of 21.5 for adult females and 22.5 for adult males.

●●Sedentary means a lifestyle that includes physical activity associated with typical day-to-day life.

●●●Moderately active means a lifestyle that includes physical activity equivalent to walking about 1.5–3 miles per day at 3–4 miles per hour, in addition to the light physical activity associated with typical day-to-day life.

●●●●Active means a lifestyle that includes physical activity equivalent to walking more than 3 miles per day at 3–4 miles per hour, in addition to the light physical activity associated with typical day-to-day life.

or unlimited quantities. Sugar is known as a simple carbohydrate and it doesn't provide the premium fuel needed for longer-lasting energy; extend this to include other forms of caloric sweeteners, such as honey, brown sugar, syrup, molasses, and so on. These all contribute calories but no other real nutrient value, if staying within an appropriate amount. Like fat, it should not be consumed in such quantity that it contributes toward a significant amount of overall daily calories; otherwise, intake should be evaluated and reduced. Sweets are usually "fun" and taste good. They can be included in a healthy eating plan in moderation. Restricting consumption of sweets to times of reward or as a source of comfort is not recommended as this can often place too much emphasis on these types of foods and actually encourage over-consumption.

Take care to moderate use of sugar substitutes as well. The calorie-free or reduced-calorie status often gives the impression that unlimited quantities are ok. Over-consumption of most anything usually means something of more healthful value may be excluded. In addition, your children may not be meeting calorie needs required for growth, if they overindulge in sweets or empty-calorie foods.

In summary, one of the keys to optimal health for kids (and adults!) is a proper balance between nutrition and activity. The key to optimal nutrition for active kids is to: 1) provide adequate fuel and hydration; 2) replenish the body during and after the event (training as well as games); and 3) present variety in texture, taste, and nutrients, and hopefully, promote a pleasant and an educational experience.

Paying the Price for a Fast-Paced Life: Childhood Obesity

Reality is: one of the traits of a soccer mom (in fact, the whole soccer family) is the busyness of most days. Hopefully, this busyness isn't necessarily a schedule of chaos, but instead, a conscious choice to make the most of each day, to truly be "present in the moment" for family and family events, career (working moms and non-working moms alike), and self-care. Unfortunately, when planning and communication fail to occur, the chaotic schedule can overcome. Self-care often becomes minimal, work and relationships can become stressed, and the toll carries on to the rest of the family.

The 1999–2000 results from National Health and Nutrition Examination Survey (NHANES) reveal that approximately 64 percent of U.S. adults fit into the overweight or obese categories. Most data reveals that total calorie intake remains fairly constant; but that macronutrient distribution (calories from carbohydrate, fat, protein) commonly fluctuates (usually fed by the latest fad diet); that most Americans feel they have valid excuses for avoiding regularly scheduled exercise; and that many, especially women, are dissatisfied with their weight and body image. Unfortunately, people want to lose weight more often to change their appearance than to improve health and lessen risk for heart disease, diabetes, and so on. Considering we, as parents, are among our children's leading role models, providers, and educators, how do these thoughts and behaviors impact them? Obviously much more strongly than we realize.

The same NHANES of 1999–2000 previously mentioned reveals that about 16 percent of children and adolescents ages 6–19 years of age are overweight, a 45 percent increase from the appromixate 11 percent reported in the NHANES III of 1988–94 and a 69 percent increase from the approximate 5 percent reported in the NHANES of 1971–74. One of the primary concerns of this data is that overweight children and adolescents are at an increased risk to become overweight adults. Additional concerns revolve around low

self-esteem, inactivity, and health problems, which ironically can be seen in underweight children and adolescents as well, leading into some alarming statistics from the National Eating Disorders Association:

- 42 percent of 1st–3rd grade girls want to be thinner (Collins, 1991).
- 81 percent of 10-year-olds are afraid of being fat (Mellin, et al, 1991).
- 51 percent of 9- and 10-year-old girls feel better about themselves if they are on a diet (Mellin et al., 1991).
- 46 percent of 9- to 11-year-olds are "sometimes" or "very often" on diets.

Listen up Parents!!

- 82 percent of their families are "sometimes" or "very often" on diets (Gustafson-Larson and Terry, 1992).
- 95 percent of all dieters will regain their lost weight in 1–5 years (Grodstein, 1996).
- 35 percent of "normal dieters" progress to pathological dieting. Of those, 20–25 percent progress to partial or full-syndrome eating disorders (Shisslak and Crago, 1995).
- 25 percent of American men and 45 percent of American women are on a diet on any given day (Smolak, 1996).
- Americans spend more than $40 billion on dieting and diet-related products each year (Smolak, 1996).

So . . . back to the question about the impact of parents' diet and activity thoughts and behaviors. There are definitely other contributing factors, but parents/guardians, you must realize you are positioned to play a leading role in modeling and teaching credible nutrition and activity behaviors. A 2003 member survey of the American Dietetic Association (ADA) revealed that 90 percent of the responding dietetics professionals felt the greatest barriers to effective prevention of excess weight among children are parents who have poor eating habits themselves, followed by parents who lack time (59 percent), and parents who lack knowledge about what healthy eating means (45 percent).

Before delving into some of the solutions to improve overall family health, a few more pertinent statistics should be reviewed. According to the

National Restaurant Association 2005 Fact Sheet, 2005 sales for commercial eating places was $326 billion; $1.3 billion on a typical day. The 2005 total sales for all commercial categories are $437 billion. Comparison to total sales in 1996 is $313 billion (about a 40 percent increase). The average household expenditure for food away from home in 2002 was $2,276, or $910 per person. Half of all adults make restaurants an essential part of their lifestyle.

All this being said, it doesn't mean parents and restaurants should accept full blame for overweight children and adolescents. It means parents should obtain nutrition and physical activity facts for themselves and their children. That way, with encouragement and support, every member of the family would be capable of making and applying appropriate choices.

Key Nutrition, Intake, and Physical Activity Recommendations

Examine the entire family's general intake, output, and eating behaviors— a balanced eating plan that includes lots of variety (in texture and taste as well as nutrients!), complemented by consistently scheduled physical activity, is the key to good health for all. Why wait for an event such as diabetes or a heart attack to decide to make healthful lifestyle changes? Unfortunately though, this is the norm. Posting attractive and educational graphics such as *MyPyramid* on the fridge is a great reminder of the foundation for healthy eating and activity. The colorful fare might serve to provide ideas for the next grocery list. Having posted definitions of various portion sizes is also convenient when loading plates and in the moments just prior to the "point-of-consumption!" Comparing each day's intake to at least the minimum recommendations of each category provides an easy way to see if nutrient and activity needs are being met. If not, you can easily identify foods/activities to incorporate.

Once you have taken a good look at your family's eating behaviors, you might consider the following:

- Establish at least one mealtime per day . . . more is great but often not realistic.
- Avoid doing any additional activities, other than engaging in pleasant conversation, while eating (i.e., reading, watching TV, lecturing on inappropriate behavior, studying, or so on).

- NEVER eat directly out of a "bulk" container. Always get "a serving/portion" and put the remainder away. Eating directly from the container, especially in conjunction with a distracting activity, can easily lead to over-consumption.
- Wait until everyone is at the table before eating begins. Eat slowly; possibly even putting flatware down between bites if speed seems to be an issue.
- Model and encourage "filling" your plate with one serving of each food item offered. After sampling from all, wait a short time before going back for seconds. If you go for seconds, go for a half serving.
- Avoid labeling food as "good" or "bad" unless you're referring to its taste, rather than its purported nutritional value.
- Discourage eating while prepping food. Sampling means putting a small amount in a clean utensil to taste-test, which is fine, especially if instructed to "season to taste." Along these same lines, avoid "cleaning up" after others. By this, we don't mean skip doing the dishes. We mean skip eating food left on others' plates.

Often we don't realize what or how much we eat until we take a good, positive look at it. The goal should be to assess and improve for good health, not to criticize or restrict for diet and weight-loss purposes. Bottom line, we all have room for improvement when it comes to nutrition and exercise; it is in everyone's best interest to not make a child feel singled out for improvement or that he/she has been put on a diet.

Encourage healthy eating the majority of the time for all; practice moderation, rather than abstinence, of foods that are higher in fat and sugar—expose children to factual and easily identified resources like *MyPyramid*. Educate your family on appropriate portion sizes. You can also reference individual product labels. With no standards in portioning, however, the labels might not always be accurate in what an actual serving should be. Consider the example of soda pop. While pop should not contribute a significant amount of calories in one's intake, as it is one of those calorie-dense items that provide empty calories, it can be included in a controlled amount. A typical serving would be 8–12 ounces. However, think about the cup sizes offered at soda fountains. Seldom do they constitute only 8 ounces. Instead, consumers are often encouraged to choose larger sizes and

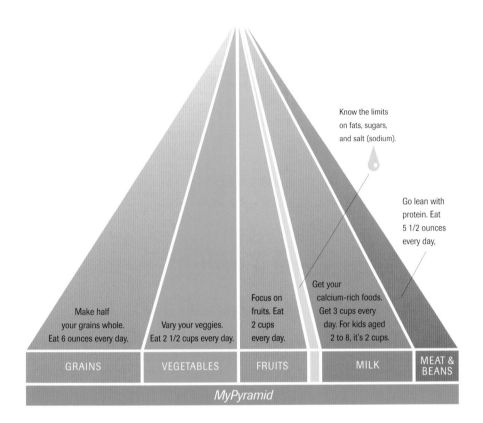

Know the limits on fats, sugars, and salt (sodium).

Go lean with protein. Eat 5 1/2 ounces every day,

Get your calcium-rich foods. Get 3 cups every day. For kids aged 2 to 8, it's 2 cups.

Focus on fruits. Eat 2 cups every day.

Make half your grains whole. Eat 6 ounces every day.

Vary your veggies. Eat 2 1/2 cups every day.

GRAINS   VEGETABLES   FRUITS   MILK   MEAT & BEANS

MyPyramid

pay one low price. Pre-packaged bottles of pop are usually 20 ounces. Look closely at the label, and the nutrition information will define the number of servings in that bottle as two. How many people buy the bottle with the intent of saving half for another time, or, sharing it with someone else? Again, for children and adults alike, learn portion sizes and make those amounts the foundation of the food consumed. An especially helpful tool is the visualization of various portion sizes.

Sugar and fats are meant to be consumed in smaller quantities, in moderation. Include children in meal-planning and prep, striving to make food experiences, as previously mentioned, nourishing, energizing, and pleasurable; at the same time, discuss how foods like sugar and fat can be included. Avoid completely eliminating any specific food item. It appears that the more frequently food is restricted or denied, the more desirable it becomes, often resulting in episodes of bingeing or overeating.

The ideal intake for most people is nutrient density over calorie density. Take for example, choosing a good source of calcium, for strong bones and teeth, from the dairy group. A serving of cheddar cheese is 1½ ounces for

Visualizing Portion Sizes

Food Group	Portion Size	Looks like . . .
Grains	1 bread slice	computer disk, Day At-A-Glance calendar page
	1 waffle or pancake	(same as above)
	1/2 cup	tennis ball, covers the palm of your hand
	1 cup	fills half of standard cereal bowl
	1 tortilla	6 inch diameter
Vegetables and Fruits	1/2 cup	covers the palm of your hand, light bulb (asparagus or broccoli)
	1 medium	tennis ball, eyeglass case (banana)
Dairy	1 ounce cheese	4 dice, 2 dominoes, computer disk
	1/2 cup cottage cheese	covers the palm of your hand
	1/2 cup ice cream	tennis ball
Protein	2 ounces	small chicken leg
	3 ounces	cassette tape or deck of cards, 1/2 large chicken breast, covers palm of your hand
	1 ounce nuts	covers palm of your hand
	2 tablespoons peanut butter	ping pong ball
Fats	2 teaspoons margarine	size of thumb

a calorie value of 165 with 13.5 grams fat, 9.1 grams saturated fat, and 204 milligrams of calcium. A serving of fruit-flavored yogurt (add your own fresh fruit for more fiber and fewer calories!) is 1 cup (8 ounces) for a calorie value of 230 with 3 grams fat, 1.8 grams saturated fat, and 343 milligrams of calcium. The yogurt obviously provides more nutrient density of the calcium for the calories, as well as total volume, unless, of course, your goal was to increase density of fat and saturated fat, which is not advisable for a healthy heart. This isn't to say cheese is bad for you. Cheese is, however, one of those foods that should be portion-controlled and included in moderation, as it is dense in fat and saturated fat.

Encourage *and* join in daily physical activity—while it can be extremely challenging to set aside a dedicated 30–90 minute timeslot each day to exercise, reality is, even short bouts of activity can be very beneficial. Including healthful behaviors such as walking two blocks to the grocery store for a few items rather than driving, parking farther back in a parking lot rather than front row, and taking the stairs over the escalator or elevator (though these are sometimes fun things to do!) all contribute to being energized rather than sedentary. While it is easy to send kids out to play, surprise them at times by including yourself in the activity. Maybe that's a good time for a walk and one-on-one conversation, or a bike ride (helmets on, of course!). Always encourage and support your kids if they choose to participate in sports. School PE isn't always available, so after-school practice and games contribute to increased activity. However, don't insist that your kids participate in organized sports. There are plenty of physical activity options available, and it's best to identify one that sparks interest and motivation rather than dread.

Practicing "all things in moderation," negotiate a budget for inactive pastimes—just as it isn't productive to label some foods as bad, the same holds true for some activities that are quite sedentary yet still very important or . . . just relaxing and fun! Therefore, establish time limits, and balance sedentary time with active time. If you include watching TV in the budget, take advantage of commercials now and then to take care of demands that require attention yet little time.

Identifying an overweight child—refrain from suggesting overweight status to a child. Realize that all children grow at different rates and periods of time. Don't intentionally restrict foods or calories. Be aware that a medically necessary, restrictive meal plan for an adult may not necessarily be the wisest preventive health care choice for children. For example, an overweight, sedentary, smoking parent surviving a heart attack will most likely be prescribed the following lifestyle changes: reduce calories, fat, saturated fat, cholesterol, and sodium intake to prescribed levels, stop smoking, and, upon clearance from the physician, begin a moderate but progressive cardio program. The goals for these recommendations are for reducing weight, addressing an abnormal cholesterol profile, controlling blood pressure, improving lung and cardiac health, and making exercise and other healthful lifestyle behaviors routine activities of daily living. Since cardiac disease of one generation automatically becomes a risk factor for future generations, the well-meaning parents may implement the restrictive meal plan for the entire family. However, rather than go to this extreme, those parents might review and apply healthful guidelines (e.g., the 2005 Dietary Guidelines) as a first step, with the goal to create positive, encouraging, and long-lasting change. Additionally, children require adequate calories and protein for growth, so do not adopt a plan that severely restricts calories/nutrients. If necessary, see a health care provider (most likely a medical doctor [M.D.] or registered dietitian [R.D.]) for the most appropriate recommendations.

Support your child and be a good listener—examine your ability to show unconditional love. Take time to give your undivided attention if your child should want to share concerns about weight or body image. Unfortunately for children and adults, food and exercise can become enemies if they are sensitive, daily issues rather than promoting healthful living as they are intended. This occurs especially with children who are constantly criticized about their food choices and eating behaviors, and ironically enough, the messages given are often quite confusing: "clean your plate," "you eat too much," "you eat too little."

Registered dietitian and therapist Ellyn Satter states in her book, *How to Get Your Kid to Eat . . . But Not Too Much,* "Parents are responsible for food shopping, preparation, serving meals, and getting everyone to the table. Then they need to stop, and trust that the child will eat what he or she needs."

Eventually, the modified adage, "Parents should be seen and not heard," might apply at mealtime, at least when it comes to food intake. Why?

Because you equip your children with tools to make their own appropriate choices when you consistently expose them to the foundations of healthy eating through conversation; through *MyPyramid* and other kid-specific, colorful educational tools; through letting them assist with meal-planning and prep; and through behaving as a mealtime role-model. You should also avoid using food as a reward, punishment, or source of comfort. When all is said and done, kids' ability to visualize portion sizes, and their normal cycle of hunger and satiety, should regulate the amount of their intake.

When it comes to children's concerns regarding exercise and eating, parents should be all ears. The fun and healthy aspects of physical activity quickly vanish if a child feels less than adequate for reasons such as being clumsy, always coming in last, never getting picked for a team, and so on. Believe it or not, all of this strongly impacts the child's future nutrition status, motivation for exercise, self-esteem, and eating behaviors. Therefore, when the opportunity arises, strive to listen and show understanding and support to the child who is less than comfortable with issues relating to food and activity.

 # Kids and Nutrition Supplementation

One of the intents of the Dietary Guidelines addressed in chapter 1 is to provide education on nutrient needs and to stress the importance of meeting these needs by way of food consumption. A general recommendation is to eat a variety of nutrient-packed foods daily.

Considering the growing statistics on overweight/obesity, you might be tempted to restrict calories and attempt to meet nutrient needs by taking a vitamin or mineral supplement. But the important nutrients missing in this scenario are the macronutrients (carbohydrate, fat, and protein), as those are the ones that contribute calories. Additionally, giving performance-enhancing supplements to children or adolescents participating in sports is not recommended.

The term supplement no longer pertains to only vitamin and mineral products. The supplementation market has grown to include herbs, botanicals, enzymes, energy bars, drinks, and more. Unfortunately, quality control comes into question because the products don't have to meet any federal standards. Wouldn't you be concerned if medicine was not subject to standardization? How could a parent feel confident that the over-the-counter or prescription drugs they were giving their child were safe, pure, of high quality, and in the proper dosage? At higher dosages, some supplements, herbs, and the like can imitate drugs, with potential side effects as minor as irritability or stomach upset or as extreme as vital organ damage or, in some cases, death. Some supplements may create problems by interacting with a prescription drug that a child may be taking.

We provide this information not to cause fear but to encourage all, prior to giving children supplements, to thoroughly educate themselves, by way of a credible source. Consider the following questions:

- Why is supplementation indicated? Have efforts to eat according to the Dietary Guidelines been exhausted? Have you spoken with and gotten a physician's blessing? Has potential conflict with prescription drugs been discussed?
- Does the label provide ingredient information as well as percentage of nutrients provided? If so, how do these percentages compare to the child's needs?
- Does the product provide child-specific dosages? Is any information noted about potential side effects or when and how the supplement needs to be taken?
- Has the supplement been tested and safely approved for kids?
- Does the product have documented evidence, from a credible source, for any claims that may be made?
- What is the cost of the product? How does this compare to the cost of obtaining the same nutrients from food?
- If the act of supplementation is to improve health, does this coincide with other healthful behaviors such as improving intake, incorporating consistent activity on a regular basis, protecting the child from second-hand smoke?

If the original intent of supplementation is to make for a healthier child, the questions above can appear off-putting, yet products available for supplementation are wide-ranging. They can be as basic as a standard multivitamin supplement or as extensive as single nutrient vitamins, minerals, or herbal products that carry a recommended dosage, many attractive claims, and the potential to be as strong as some prescription drugs. Those targeted at kids come in various shapes, sizes, flavors, and even popular cartoon characters (which begs the questions, do younger children see these as candy or treats, and are they safely stored so little hands can't locate and eat them as if they were candy?). They may also send the message that children don't have to worry about making healthy food choices, as their supplement will provide all they need.

In conclusion, children should not be the target of these products, and ideally, a healthcare provider should be the one to identify need for supplementation and to recommend the optimal product. The American Academy of Pediatrics strongly condemns the use of performance-enhancing

substances and vigorously endorses efforts to eliminate their use among children and adolescents. The preference remains to meet nutrient needs through healthy food consumption. If the backup security of a multivitamin supplement is desired, read the product label and strive to find one that meets no more than 100 percent of the recommended daily needs.

 # Fast Food Fiestas . . . Friend or Foe?

With common sense as your guide, you can incorporate most edibles in a healthy lifestyle . . . IN MODERATION!!!! Yes, this even includes fast food! Fast food restaurants take quite a beating, possibly one of the reasons why the restaurant industry refers to them as "quick service" restaurants; actually, quick service also includes limited-service and snack and nonalcoholic beverage bars. They are viewed positively in the industry for their ability to meet consumer desires for value and convenience, including the addition of credit card options. Reported sales increased 4.4 percent from 2003–2004 (from $136 billion to $142.5 billion). These statistics make the negative connotations that many consumers attach to fast food rather paradoxical since the law of supply and demand usually dictates what survives; it has been said that menu trends are driven by consumer demand. The National Restaurant Association (NRA) strives to be an industry of "choice" and to meet their objective of accommodating the diverse needs of a diverse population. Additionally, it prides itself on cooperative alliances with groups such as the American Dietetic Association (ADA) and the American Council for Fitness and Nutrition (ACFN) as partners in addressing health concerns.

In short order, so to speak, the 900,000 full-service and quick-service restaurants reported on the NRA 2005 Fact Sheet obviously exist as a result of demand. Their menus include a wide variety of food and beverage items, in every aspect imaginable, including those modified to address consumer health interests such as low-fat, low-carbohydrate, and so on. And due to alliances formed with groups such as the ADA and ACFN, many restaurants support and participate in community health promotion activities.

The point isn't to promote the NRA but, rather, to acknowledge that as busy families, as well as individuals (young and elderly alike), we obviously like the variety and convenience this industry provides. Rather than blame them for our increasing weight statistics, it would be more productive to realize the emphasis should be placed on individual choice. Therefore, keeping the Dietary Guidelines in mind, obtain the nutrition facts (which many

operations provide), and make appropriate choices based on personal needs and preferences.

Other important fast food dining considerations:

Frequency—While eating out can be fun and a true convenience, high-frequency shouldn't be the norm. If it is, it can be costly for health as well as the pocketbook! Cooking and eating at home is a good experience for everyone involved. It can serve as an educational opportunity, especially for kids, in terms of menu-planning, making shopping lists, cooking, learning portion sizes, trying new foods, and serving as part of the set-up and clean-up crew. It also allows for great conversation when busy schedules don't appear to allow for this!

Incorporation into the day's/week's total intake—Plan ahead (or afterward) to find a reasonable way to include meals of higher calorie density. This doesn't mean intake should be drastically restricted to include fast food. In fact, we don't recommend that you omit meals to "save up" for one. Rather, complementary meals could focus on providing nutrient density and food groups that might otherwise be missing. As shown in the "Fast Food Choices to Consider" example, it's easy to overlook the fruit group, so the complementary meals would be a good opportunity to meet serving recommendations. Additionally, many fast food restaurants now offer more fruit options; however, they won't supply what isn't demanded.

Mealtime location—Family mealtime should take place seated around the table, not driving down the street. Therefore, avoid "drive-through/ drive-away dining" (although reality may sometimes dictate, so moderation can be the key here too!). The drive-through is a great convenience, but try to take the food to a traditional mealtime setting if at all possible.

Portion sizes—Maybe the kids' meal is adequate for adults, just as the extra large size may make sense if shared. Fact or fiction, it often seems the less expensive the food, the more you get; and the converse. Regardless, let the normal state of hunger participate in selections, but eat slowly enough to stop before feeling stuffed, even if there is food left. Yes, there are starving children all around the world, but there are also alternatives to overeating with this as an excuse. Take it to go, share it with someone that didn't get enough, and/or consider ordering less next time.

Fast Food Choices to Consider

For many, a typical meal might be:

Double quarter-pound cheeseburger (Two 4-ounce patties with two 1-ounce slices of American cheese plus hamburger bun) = 730 calories, 40 grams fat

Large fries (6 ounces) = 520 calories, 25 grams fat

Large soda pop (32 ounces) = 310 calories, 0 grams fat

Total meal contribution
(no condiments included)

1,560 calories, 65 grams fat, which is about 38 percent of total calories. WOW! This is one meal; it may easily consume more than 3/4 of the day's calorie and fat needs for many people! Food groups represented are grain, vegetable (more than one serving and "expensive" in terms of percentage of daily allowance for fat and calories they eat up, since most veggies are high-carbohydrate and fat-free); meat (x2! Recommendation is 4–6 ounces of lean meat per day), dairy. No fruit and minimal fiber.

Better choice

Cheeseburger (2-ounce patty with 1 ounce American cheese plus bun) = 310 calories, 12 grams fat

Small fries (2.6 ounces) = 230 calories, 11 grams fat

Child-size (NORMAL size!) soda pop (12 ounces) = 115 calories, no fat

Total meal contribution
(no condiments included)

655 calories, 23 grams fat, which is about 32 percent of total calories. Food groups represented are grain, (expensive!) veggie, meat, about half dairy. Still no fruit and minimal fiber.

Another alternative if you have someone to share with, especially if you like a thicker patty:

Quarter-pound cheeseburger **with special request** of 1 slice cheese (4-ounce patty, 1 ounce cheese [which saves 110 calories and 9 grams fat], bun) = total: 400 calories, 15 grams fat; shared: 200 calories, 8 grams fat

Medium fries (4 ounces) = 350 calories, 16 grams fat; shared: 175 calories, 8 grams fat

Child-size soda pop (12 ounces) = 115 calories, no fat

Total meal contribution
(no condiments included)

490 calories, 16 grams fat which is about 30 percent of total calories. Food groups represented: 1 grain, (calorie-dense) veggie, meat, about half dairy. Still no fruit and minimal fiber.

NOTE: While none of the above included condiments, there are several to choose from that can complement food without adding significant calories in a standard portion (usually varies from 2 teaspoons–2 tablespoons). Optimally, condiments should always be requested "on the side" so that portion size can be controlled to individual preferences.

Quality and taste discrimination—Don't settle for anything substandard in either category. Personal preferences should dictate and cheers to that! Make special requests based upon those personal preferences.

Denial—Avoid denying what is really desired when eating out. While the NRA reports an increase in requests for entrée salads, bottled water, poultry, and vegetable and fruit side dishes, don't choose these items "to be good" or in an attempt to be "healthy," if you would prefer to eat something else (in, of course, an appropriate portion). Denial, deprivation, or restriction often results in lack of fulfillment and satisfaction, with a possible binge down the road. As the NRA *Nutrition and Healthy Lifestyles* publication says, "Healthful eating patterns are not created or destroyed by one meal or one food."

"More for the money!"—Avoid this train of thought for adults and children alike when eating out. This often encourages overeating and, if done on a frequent basis, may end up costing even more in terms of health care dollars. Buffets or smorgasbords are not an excuse to eat to excess. Their value lies in their options from all food groups, great variety within those food groups, and point-of-purchase benefits.

For the athlete—If you time eating out to be either preceding or following the event (training or competition), you need to consider the special needs of fueling and replenishment. If you are simply dodging meal-planning duties, this would not be the time to go. However, since you must commonly travel with sports teams and eat out, you should take care to select foods that offer plenty of carbohydrate and lesser amounts of fat. Pre-game fueling in particular should be low-fat. If you don't have a basic knowledge of food composition in terms of carbohydrate, fat, and protein, ask for nutritional analysis information, if available. Traditional breakfast foods are usually high-carbohydrate and low-fat if extra fat isn't added or the product isn't fried. Choose from bread and grain foods such as pancakes, English muffins, and bagels. Add one serving of egg or a lean meat to round out an appropriate amount of protein, especially if complemented by a serving of low-fat milk. Avoid potatoes or hash browns that are deep fried or cooked with lots of extra fat as a pre-game food source. Whenever fruit or fruit juice is available, that is a good choice (but continue to control portion size if pre-game). For lunch and dinner, look for menu items that are high in carbohydrate and low in fat as well (again, reference nutritional analysis information if necessary). Choose lean meats (or substitutes), pastas, rice, and other grains, as well as beans, potatoes, and other vegetables, avoiding fried foods and heavy sauces in particular, at this time. Refueling might be the time to include cold and refreshing treats like ice cream, frozen yogurt, sherbet, and such.

In summary, to complement a realistic and healthy lifestyle, quick service restaurants can be an appropriate and positive option, in moderation and depending on choices made.

 # Fruitful Fueling: Pre-Game Foods

Carbohydrates are the premium fuel for pre-game (the days leading up to as well as the day of), during the game, and post-game. As previously noted, it is recommended that 55–75 percent of total calories come from carbohydrate so that fuel reserves provide for best performance. Carbohydrate choices recommended for inclusion on a daily basis include a variety of whole grain breads, cereals, and pastas as well as a variety of fruits and vegetables. While higher-fiber choices are usually best, pre-game might be a time to include the lower-fiber grains, fruits, and veggies so as to avoid problems with bloating or cramping. However, someone that consumes high fiber on a regular basis might not experience negative side effects. While fat and protein should contribute to the meal, fried foods and heavy sauces should be avoided and protein should only contribute about one serving (equivalent of 2 ounces).

Mealtime should occur 2–4 hours prior to the event, and, if you're counting, provide about 75–200 grams carbohydrate (an example might be: 1 whole English muffin (27 grams), 2 tablespoons peanut butter (14 grams), 2 tablespoons apple butter (12 grams), 1 cup low-fat milk (1 percent fat; 14 grams), and 1 medium banana (27 grams) for a grand total of 94 grams carbohydrate!). You might also include sport drinks. Avoid those that are highly concentrated or use only fructose as a sweetener as they may cause the stomach to feel overly full.

Also, choose from foods and beverages that you know are liked and well-tolerated. Game day is not the best time to introduce something new! Keep track of what's eaten, and you might have some food for thought, so to speak, after the game. Did the meal seem to work well? Were all foods tolerated? Did energy hold out? If there appeared to be problems, look at making changes and don't neglect to consider intake on the days leading up to the event.

PRE-GAME BREAKFASTS
"Fast Break" Breakfast Wrap 'n' Roll

SERVES 4

1 tablespoon canola oil
2 cups shredded potatoes
Salt and pepper, to taste
¼ cup bacon bits
3 eggs, beaten
2 tablespoons water
½ teaspoon dry mustard
4 flour tortillas
4 tablespoons grated sharp
   cheddar cheese
Salsa, optional

Guaranteed to put an extra bounce in your child's step! Customize this to your preferences. Serve with some fresh fruit for optimal carbohydrate input.

Heat canola oil in a skillet over medium heat. Add shredded potatoes and cook about 15 minutes until tender. Add salt and pepper to taste. Sprinkle bacon bits atop potatoes and reduce heat to low while prepping eggs.

In a small bowl, beat eggs, water, and dry mustard. Turn heat under skillet to medium high and pour eggs over all. Gently stir and cook through. Remove from heat. Place ¾–1 cup of egg-potato mixture in center of each tortilla. Sprinkle 1 tablespoon cheddar over each and microwave 20 seconds, until cheese has melted. Remove and fold each tortilla like a burrito. Serve with salsa, if desired.

PER SERVING: 374 calories, 39 grams carbohydrate, 17.8 grams fat, 14.6 grams protein.

"Breakaway" Breakfast Subs

SERVES 2

1 hoagie bun (6 inch)
1 ounce slice ham, cut in
    ½ to fit on bun
2 scrambled eggs, seasoned
    to taste
1 ounce slice provolone cheese,
    cut in ½ to fit on bun

You can never go WRONG with a great-tasting sub. These are yummy as-is, but you may add what you like to dress them up. If your condiments are high-fat, use in moderation.

Assemble subs in the ingredient order listed. Place in a toaster oven and toast for 2–3 minutes. Remove from oven, halve, and serve.

PER ½ SUB: 347 calories,
 77.4 grams carbohydrate,
14.5 grams fat, 15.3 grams protein.

BREAKAWAY:

a one-on-one showdown between a sole attacker and goalkeeper

"Manchester in the Morning"
aka English Muffin Sandwich

SERVES 1

1 teaspoon canola margarine
½ ounce diced ham
1 egg, beaten with 1 tablespoon
    water and ¼ teaspoon
    dry mustard
Salt and pepper to taste
½ tablespoon shredded
    mozzarella cheese
1 white or whole wheat
    English muffin
½ tablespoon shredded sharp
    cheddar cheese

In this fast food "knock-off" with a healthier twist, using a combo of the two cheeses reduces the fat by half. Salsa is a nice complement.

Melt margarine in a skillet over medium high heat. Stir in ham and sauté for 1 minute. Pour the egg into the ham and mix; season. Cook for 2 minutes over medium heat, stirring as needed. Remove from heat. Spoon cooked egg-ham mixture on one English muffin half. Sprinkle with cheese. Top with other muffin half, and microwave for 15–20 seconds to melt cheese.

PER SANDWICH: 279 calories,
26.3 grams carbohydrate,
12.4 grams fat, 15.7 grams protein.

MANCHESTER UNITED:

(often abbreviated to Man United or just Man U) is an English football club based at Old Trafford in Greater Manchester.

"Free Kick" Fruity Yogurt Parfait

1 cup of your favorite
   low-fat yogurt
1 cup fresh fruit (like "Carry"
   Berry Mix, page 53)
2 tablespoons Post Grape-Nuts
   (1 tablespoon per layer
   yogurt), optional

Light and refreshing, adding Grape-Nuts contributes those great whole grains!

For fun, use a parfait cup or sundae dish (if not available, use a regular 6–8 ounce glass). Layer with ½ cup yogurt, ½ cup fruit, Grape-Nuts, and repeat.

PER SERVING: 303 calories, 54.3 grams carbohydrate, 3.7 grams fat, 13.1 grams protein.

Some other options:

- For some crunch, add 1 tablespoon Grape-Nuts after each yogurt layer; eat soon if you want it really crunchy. Softened, they still add some texture.
- After washing the unpeeled fruit, add ½ teaspoon lemon, orange, or lime zest to the yogurt.
- If the yogurt isn't as sweet as you'd like, sprinkle ½ teaspoon brown sugar after each yogurt layer. Just a ½ teaspoon, though. This isn't dessert!!
- Try a Citrus Yogurt Parfait—use orange crème yogurt, then layer a mix of mandarin orange, and grapefruit sections.
- Try a Berry Lime Parfait—use Key lime yogurt, then layer fresh, sliced strawberries.
- Try a Blueberry Lemon Parfait—use lemon yogurt, then layer fresh blueberries.
- For banana lovers—banana yogurt with sliced bananas; sprinkle on 1 tablespoon crushed graham crackers for variety.
- Make your own scrumptious parfait combos—let your taste be your guide!

PER SERVING (with 2 tablespoons Grape-Nuts): 355 calories, 66 grams carbohydrate, 4 grams fat, 13.9 grams protein.

FREE KICK:

an uncontested kick awarded to a player for a foul committed by an opposing player. The player kicks a stationary ball without any opposing players within 10 yards of her.

"Offsides" Oatmeal with Fruit

SERVES 2

1¾ cups water
1 cup old-fashioned oats
1 tablespoon dried cranberries
1 teaspoon brown sugar
1 cup low-fat milk (1 percent fat)

Hot cereals are packED with nutrients, especially if you replace half the cooking water with milk. Oatmeal, however, is the best of the huddle for heart health.

Bring 1 quart water to boil in a saucepan over high heat. Stir in oats and cranberries; cook 5 minutes over medium heat, stirring occasionally. Cover; remove from heat. Stir in brown sugar. Serve with ½ cup milk per serving.

PER SERVING (with ½ cup milk): 227 calories, 38.1 grams carbohydrate, 4.3 grams fat, 9 grams protein.

"Penalty" PB & J Bagel

SERVES 2

1 bagel (preferably whole grain),
    cut in half
2 tablespoons peanut butter
2 tablespoons jam or preserves
    (flavor of choice)

We call this the "penalty," because, while this recipe may not be so creative, it's still a kick to make and eat. It is also a wonderful and easy pre-game or pre-practice source of energy. Choose preserves or jam over jelly, as the latter is strained, therefore, no fiber.

Toast bagel. Spread 1 tablespoon peanut butter on each half. Top with jam or preserves.

PER ½ BAGEL: 270 calories, 38.7 grams carbohydrate, 8.9 grams fat, 8.7 grams protein.

"Yellow Card" Pineapple Slush

SERVES 5

6 ounces frozen pineapple-
    banana-orange juice
    concentrate, thawed
1 cup low-fat vanilla yogurt
½ cup low-fat milk (1 percent fat)
½ cup water
2 tablespoons sugar
1 teaspoon vanilla extract
Crushed ice

Not enough by itself, hence the "yellow card" classification, but . . . it gets the day started with an event no more than an hour or so away.

Combine all ingredients except the ice in a blender. Process until smooth. Add enough ice to raise level to 5 cups on blender; process. Serve immediately.

PER SERVING: 142 calories, 29.8 grams carbohydrate, .9 grams fat, 3.8 grams protein.

YELLOW CARD:

a playing card-sized card that a referee holds up to warn a player for unsportsmanlike conduct. 2 yellow cards = an automatic red card, meaning ejection from the game.

"Shutout" Strawberry-Banana-Kiwi Smoothie

SERVES 4

1 small ripe banana, peeled and cut
   into chunks
1 ½ cups sliced strawberries
   (preferably fresh, but frozen
   is ok)
1 kiwi fruit, peeled, chopped
8 ounces strawberry
   low-fat yogurt
¾ cup low-fat milk (1 percent fat)

Always a great choice. Then again, there are so many choices with smoothies! Pick the combos you like best.

Combine all ingredients in a blender. Process until smooth. Serve immediately.

PER SERVING: 133 calories, 24.5 grams carbohydrate, 1.6 grams fat, 5.3 grams protein.

"Carry" Berry Mix

SERVES 8

1 quart fresh strawberries, sliced
1 cup fresh blueberries
1 cup fresh blackberries
1 cup fresh raspberries

CARRY:

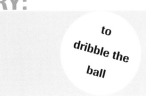

to dribble the ball

Fresh, rinsed berries are best, but in a pinch, frozen are ok. Leftovers can be used for a smoothie!

Gently combine the first 3 berries. Lightly toss with the raspberries.

PER SERVING: 57 calories, 12 grams carbohydrate, 0.6 grams fat, 0.8 grams protein.

PRE-GAME LUNCHES
"Play On" Pizza Bagels

SERVES 2

1 bagel (try the Everything or
    Asiago cheese flavors)
2 tablespoons tomato paste
2 slices provolone cheese
    (1 ounce each)

What child doesn't love pizza?
Add other veggies or lean
protein, such as chopped bell
peppers, sliced mushrooms,
and/or shredded chicken breast,
for variety.

Lightly toast bagel. Remove from
oven and spread each bagel half
with 1 tablespoon tomato paste.
Lay 1 slice of cheese over tomato
paste on each bagel. Place bagel
halves under broiler until cheese
melts and is lightly browned.

PER ½ BAGEL: 231 calories,
26.5 grams carbohydrate,
8.3 grams fat, 12.4 grams protein.

"Red Card" Canned Fruit Mix

SERVES 10

1 can (20 ounces) pineapple
   chunks, drained, juice reserved
   for later use
1 can (11 ounces) mandarin
   orange sections, drained
1 can (15 ounces) sliced peaches,
   in fruit juice, cut in chunks
1 can (15 ounces) pear halves,
   in fruit juice, cut in chunks
2 tablespoons pineapple-banana-
   orange juice concentrate, thawed

Moms, we know you can do better, but sometimes a hectic day can sideline you, and you really need something right now. Again, canned is not as nutrient-rich as fresh but it's better than none.

Combine fruits; toss with juice concentrate. Chill and serve.

PER SERVING: 98 calories,
23.7 grams carbohydrate,
0 grams fat, 0.9 grams protein.

RED CARD:

a playing card-sized card that a referee holds up to signal a player's removal from the game for unsportsmanlike conduct or multiple rule infractions. (two yellow cards = one red card).

"Chip Pass"
Chicken and Pasta

SERVES 6

1 teaspoon olive oil
1 clove garlic, minced
2 tablespoons white
   cooking wine
1 teaspoon salt
3 boneless, skinless chicken breasts,
   thinly sliced into pieces
½ cup chicken broth
1 tablespoon cornstarch
6 cups cooked pasta (choose
   a fun shape, like campanelle
   or farfalle; cooked according
   to package directions)
Parmesan cheese, optional

This recipe is ripe for customizing, with lots of potential for more veggies. It's fun to use several varieties of pasta at once, as well.

Combine first 4 ingredients in a bowl or storage bag. Add chicken and marinate about 30 minutes. Drain chicken then sauté in a heated skillet over medium heat.

Meanwhile, heat chicken broth and stir in cornstarch; cook until thickened. Toss chicken with pasta then pour broth over all. Stir gently to coat. Serve with shredded Parmesan cheese, if desired.

PER SERVING (with 1 cup pasta): 288 calories, 41.3 grams carbohydrate, 4 grams fat, 21.6 grams protein.

CHIP PASS:

a pass lofted into the air from a player to a teammate.

"Gooooooooooooal-icious"
Chicken Quesadillas

SERVES 8

¼ cup rice wine vinegar

½ tablespoon soy sauce

½ teaspoon brown sugar

1 clove garlic, minced

1 teaspoon sesame oil

2 raw boneless, skinless
  chicken breasts, thinly sliced

1 cup sliced mushrooms, optional

Canola or olive oil
  cooking spray

¼ cup shredded Colby
  Jack cheese

¼ cup shredded
  mozzarella cheese

8 flour tortillas

Salsa, optional

Low-fat sour cream, optional

These South-of-the-Border-inspired wedges deserve a victory shout for their blend of lean protein, carbs, and fat.

Combine first 5 ingredients in a bowl; mix well. Add chicken pieces; stir to cover. Refrigerate chicken at least 30 minutes or until ready to use.

After marinating, drain chicken from liquid and sauté in a heated skillet over high heat, stirring constantly. After cooking chicken about 2 minutes, add sliced mushrooms and sauté until chicken is lightly browned. Remove from heat.

Begin heating a griddle sprayed lightly with nonstick cooking spray over medium high heat.

Combine the 2 shredded cheeses and mix well. Spread ½ cup chicken/mushroom mixture on a tortilla and sprinkle with 2 tablespoons cheese blend. Place a second tortilla on top of the mixture. Transfer to the preheated griddle. Brown each side, about 1–2 minutes, then flip. Remove quesadilla to a cutting board and cut into six wedges. Great served with salsa and low-fat sour cream.

PER SERVING: 201 calories, 21.5 grams carbohydrate, 7.7 grams fat, 11.6 grams protein.

GOOOOOOOOOAL:

the signature call of sportscaster, Andrea Cantora.

"Championship" Cod 'n' Veggie Bake

SERVES 6

Canola or olive oil
   cooking spray
1½ pounds cod, cut into
   6 portions
¼ cup lemon juice
2 tablespoons red onion, minced
2 Roma tomatoes, chopped
2 teaspoons fresh dill
¼ teaspoon salt
Black pepper, to taste
½ cup shredded
   mozzarella cheese

Not many carbohydrates here but a good, lean source of protein. Therefore, complement it with something of high-carb density, such as steamed brown rice.

Preheat oven to 350°F. Spray a 9-inch x 13-inch baking dish with nonstick cooking spray. Place cod in dish and pour lemon juice over all; set aside.

Combine the onion and tomatoes; sprinkle over fish. Season by sprinkling the dill, salt, and pepper over fish and veggies. Top with cheese. Bake for 30 minutes.

PER SERVING: 159 calories,
3.2 grams carbohydrate,
2.8 grams fat, 30.4 grams protein.

"World Cup" Veggie Bake

SERVES 10

2 cups baby carrots
1 cup fresh green beans, cut into ½
 inch pieces
Canola or olive oil cooking spray
1 cup fresh mushrooms, sliced
¼ teaspoon minced garlic
1 teaspoon margarine
½ teaspoon dried basil
¼ teaspoon onion powder
¼ teaspoon salt
Dash pepper
1 cup grape tomatoes (or cherry
 tomatoes, sliced in half)
¼ cup shredded sharp
 cheddar cheese
½ cup shredded mozzarella cheese

Lots of color and nutrient variety. Expand on it if desired, and add some spinach to remind you of a springy green "pitch!"

Preheat oven to 350°F. Cook carrots and beans until crisp-tender (in boiling water, steam, or microwave); drain. Spray a 2-quart casserole dish with nonstick cooking oil. Place veggies in dish; set aside.

In another pan, sauté mushrooms and garlic in margarine; add basil, onion powder, salt, and pepper. Remove from heat and pour over carrots and beans. Drop tomatoes atop veggies. Sprinkle with both cheeses. Bake for 15–20 minutes.

PER SERVING: 52 calories,
4.8 grams carbohydrate,
2.4 grams fat, 3 grams protein.

"Champions" Corn Chowder

SERVES 8

3 cups shredded potatoes,
    fresh, frozen, or refrigerated,
    with no added salt
1 can (14.75 ounces) cream corn
2 cups frozen corn,
    no added salt
1 can (14.75 ounces) lima
    beans, drained
1½ cups water
1½ cups low-fat milk
    (1 percent fat)
¼ teaspoon onion powder
½ teaspoon salt, or season
    to taste
Dash pepper

This chowder is an amazing
source of fiber.

In a 4-quart stockpot, combine
first 4 ingredients and toss gently.
Stir in water, milk, and seasonings.
Simmer about 20 minutes, or until
heated through.

PER SERVING: 218 calories,
43.1 grams carbohydrate,
1.9 grams fat, 7.5 grams protein.

"Sweeper" Shells

SERVES 1

1 cup pasta shells, cooked
¾ cup tomato sauce
2 tablespoons shredded
    cheddar cheese

Quick and easy! Lots of carbs without much fat.

Combine shells and tomato sauce. Heat about 30 seconds in the microwave to warm sauce. Sprinkle cheese on top.

PER SERVING: 337 calories,
53.4 grams carbohydrate,
7.7 grams fat, 13.5 grams protein.

SWEEPER:
the defender that plays closest to his own goal behind the rest of the defenders. The Sweeper is a team's last line of defense in front of the goalkeeper.

"Striker" Spanish Rice and Black Beans

SERVES 8

Canola or olive oil
    cooking spray
1 pound lean ground beef
    (preferably 93 percent lean)
¼ teaspoon onion powder
1 can (15 ounces) crushed
    tomatoes
4 ounces tomato sauce
1 cup water
¾ cup rice, uncooked
1 teaspoon salt
1 teaspoon brown sugar
½ teaspoon cumin
1 can (15 ounces) black beans,
    drained, rinsed
½ cup shredded Colby Jack cheese
Salsa, optional

Save for later if beans are a problem but . . . work on increasing fiber intake away from game day, if possible.

Preheat oven to 375°F. Spray a 2-quart baking pan with nonstick cooking spray. Brown beef; drain. Stir in next 8 ingredients. Simmer 25–30 minutes over low heat. Stir in black beans. Place mixture in the baking pan and sprinkle with the cheese. Bake about 10 minutes. Serve with salsa, if desired.

PER SERVING: 277 calories, 34.2 grams carbohydrate, 6.8 grams fat, 19.8 grams protein.

STRIKER:

a team's best scorer who plays toward the center of the field.

"Playoff" Pasta and Turkey Salad

SERVES 8

DRESSING:

1 cup low-fat buttermilk

½ cup low-fat plain yogurt

¼ cup reduced-fat mayonnaise

1 package (.4 ounces) Ranch
   Salad Dressing mix

SALAD:

2 cups dry rotini pasta

1 cup chopped smoked turkey

1 cup chopped fresh broccoli

½ cup shredded carrots

¼ cup shredded
   Parmesan cheese

Light and refreshing. It works just as well with less dressing, if you prefer.

Combine the first 4 ingredients and chill at least 30 minutes.

In a 2-quart saucepan, bring water to a boil. Cook pasta, according to package directions; drain. Combine the cooked pasta, turkey, broccoli, and carrots. Toss to blend. Pour up to 1 cup dressing over all and lightly toss to blend. Chill at least 2 hours prior to serving. Just before serving, sprinkle the cheese on top and toss.

PER SERVING: 103 calories, 9.6 grams carbohydrate, 3.4 grams fat, 8.7 grams protein.

PRE-GAME DINNERS

"MVP" Broccoli and Cauliflower Au Gratin

SERVES 12

Canola or olive oil
    cooking spray
3 cups fresh cauliflower florets
3 cups fresh broccoli florets
2 teaspoons melted canola
    margarine
Dash onion powder
¼ teaspoon salt
½ cup shredded mozzarella cheese
¼ cup shredded sharp
    cheddar cheese
⅓ cup reduced-fat sour cream
½ cup breadcrumbs

Serve with a higher-carb dish, such as brown rice, to get maximum gain.

Preheat oven to 350°F. Spray a 2-quart casserole dish with nonstick cooking spray; set aside. Steam cauliflower and broccoli until crisp tender; place in a bowl after cooking.

Meanwhile, combine remaining ingredients, except the breadcrumbs. Pour over the veggies and toss gently. Sprinkle with the breadcrumbs. Bake for 30 minutes, or until heated through.

PER ½ CUP SERVING: 72 calories, 6.8 grams carbohydrate, 3 grams fat, 4.1 grams protein.

"Chargin'" Chili Joes

SERVES 8

1 pound lean ground beef
   (preferably about
   93 percent lean)
1 tablespoon minced onion
8 ounces tomato sauce
1 tablespoon brown sugar
1 teaspoon mustard
½ teaspoon garlic powder
½ teaspoon chili powder
1 can (15 ounces) red
   kidney bean
Salt and pepper, to taste
8 hamburger buns

This saucy sandwich is a cross between a chili dog and a Sloppy Joe.

Brown beef and onion; drain. Return to skillet and stir in tomato sauce, sugar, mustard, and garlic and chili powders. Add kidney beans and stir gently. Season to taste. Spoon about ½ cup of the mixture on each of the buns.

PER SANDWICH: 260 calories, 33 grams carbohydrate, 6.4 grams fat, 17.8 grams protein.

CHARGE:

to run into an opponent. It's permitted if done from the front or side of the ball carrier. It's a penalty to charge into a player without the ball or from behind.

"Drop Kick" Chicken and Veggie Stir-fry

1 tablespoon soy sauce

½ teaspoon sesame oil

¼ teaspoon garlic powder

1 teaspoon cornstarch

Dash pepper

1 pound boneless, skinless
     chicken breast, sliced into
     2-inch x 1-inch pieces

¾ cup chicken broth

2 tablespoons cornstarch

2 tablespoons cold water

2 tablespoons sesame oil

1 teaspoon minced garlic

2 green onions, diagonally sliced
     into ½ inch pieces

1 pound fresh mushrooms, cut
     in quarters

¾ cup shredded carrots

1 cup broccoli florets, chopped

1 can (8 ounces) sliced water
     chestnuts, drained

4 cups brown rice, cooked

A great dish for the whole family, and makes wonderful leftovers. We like it with brown rice or whole wheat noodles.

To prepare the marinade, combine first 5 ingredients; mix well. Place chicken breast in a glass bowl and pour marinade over the top; stirring so all chicken is coated. Cover and refrigerate until ready to use.

In a small bowl, combine chicken broth, cornstarch, and cold water; set aside.

Heat 1 tablespoon sesame oil in a skillet over high heat. Sauté garlic, onion, and mushrooms about 2 minutes. Add the chicken (drained) and continue to stir-fry until the chicken is cooked through. Remove the chicken and veggies; set aside. Add remaining 1 tablespoon sesame oil to the skillet and place over high heat. Stir-fry the carrots and broccoli for 3 minutes, or until crisp-tender. Return the chicken and veggies to the skillet and stir in the reserved broth mixture. Add the water chestnuts. Cook and stir until the broth is thickened. Serve over cooked rice.

PER SERVING (with ½ cup rice): 254 calories, 34 grams carbohydrate, 5 grams fat, 18.1 grams protein.

DROP KICK:

the action of the goalkeeper dropping the ball from her hands then kicking it just after it hits the ground.

"Hat Trick" Cornbread and Beef Casserole

SERVES 8

Canola or olive oil
    cooking spray
1 pound lean ground beef
    (preferably about
    93 percent lean)
¼ teaspoon onion powder
¼ teaspoon garlic powder
1¼ teaspoons salt
1 cup cornmeal
½ teaspoon baking soda
½ cup egg substitute, such as
    Egg Beaters
7 ounces whole kernel
    corn, drained
1 cup creamed corn
¼ cup plus 2 tablespoons
    shredded sharp
    cheddar cheese
¾ cup shredded
    mozzarella cheese
Salsa, optional

Covers three food groups: protein, grain, and veggie. Complement with fruit and a glass of milk, or a "Free Kick" Fruity Yogurt Parfait (page 49) for dessert, and you're set!

Preheat oven to 450°F. Spray the bottom of a 9-inch x 13-inch pan with nonstick cooking spray; set aside. Brown ground beef; drain. Season with onion powder, garlic powder, and ½ teaspoon salt; set aside.

Combine cornmeal, baking soda, and remaining ¾ teaspoon salt. Add egg substitute, corn, and creamed corn. Stir until just moistened.

Combine the cheddar and mozzarella in a separate bowl. Pour half of cornmeal mixture into the baking pan and spread to cover. Sprinkle with the ground beef followed by all of the cheese, except for the 2 tablespoons of sharp cheddar. Spread the remaining cornbread mixture over the beef and cheese. Bake 15–20 minutes; sprinkle the 2 tablespoons of sharp cheddar on top and bake 5 minutes more (the top should be lightly browned). Cut into 8 squares and serve. Serve with salsa, if desired.

PER SERVING: 274 calories, 27 grams carbohydrate, 9 grams fat, 21.4 grams protein.

HAT TRICK:

three or more goals scored in a game by a single player.

"Goal Kick" Grilled Pork Tenderloin

SERVES 10

½ cup white cooking wine
⅓ cup soy sauce
½ cup water
1 tablespoon sesame oil
½ teaspoon ginger
2 teaspoons minced garlic
2 tablespoons brown sugar
1 teaspoon liquid smoke
2 pounds pork tenderloin

Great flavor and surprisingly light. Needs high-carb companions, such as steamed green beans and mashed potatoes or cooked, glazed carrots.

To prepare the marinade, combine the first 8 ingredients in a bowl, reserving. Place the tenderloin in a Ziploc bag. Pour the bowl of reserved marinade over the meat. Seal the bag and refrigerate with the seal to the top; all meat should be saturated in the marinade. Chill at least 3 hours.

Preheat grill 15 minutes. Drain tenderloins then place on grill. Close lid and cook 20–25 minutes, or until internal temperature reaches 160°F on a meat thermometer. Remove from grill and cut into 1-inch slices.

PER 3 OUNCE SERVING: 140 calories, 5.7 grams carbohydrate, 4.5 grams fat, 19.2 grams protein.

GOAL KICK:

a type of restart where the ball is kicked from inside the goal area away from the goal; awarded to the defending team when a ball that crossed the goal line was last touched by a player on the attacking team.

"Lead Pass" Lasagna Sub

SERVES 7

¾ pound lean ground beef
   (preferably 93 percent lean)
1 can (8 ounces) tomato sauce
1 can (6 ounces) tomato paste
2 tablespoons red cooking wine
2 tablespoons water
¼ teaspoon oregano
¼ teaspoon basil
¼ teaspoon minced garlic
1 teaspoon salt
Dash pepper
¼ cup egg substitute, such as
   Egg Beaters
¾ cup low-fat ricotta cheese
½ cup shredded
   mozzarella cheese
1 loaf (16 ounces) French bread,
   such as a baguette
4 tablespoons grated
   Parmesan cheese

Good for on-the-go, even though it's best to have time to sit down and enjoy the meal.

Preheat the oven to 400°F. Brown the ground beef; drain and set aside.

Combine the tomato sauce, tomato paste, cooking wine, and water; mix well. Stir the tomato mixture into the browned beef. Add the oregano, basil, garlic, salt, and pepper. Simmer, covered, over low heat about 15 minutes, stirring periodically (or in microwave on power 3, for 6 minutes, stirring halfway through).

Meanwhile, combine the egg substitute, ricotta, and mozzarella; set aside. Cut the bread in half and hollow out the centers, leaving about ½ inch of the crust, sides, and bottom. Spoon half of the meat mixture into each bread half. Pour all of the cheese mixture over the meat. Cover with the remaining meat. Place each bread half on a large piece of foil, sprayed with nonstick cooking spray. Bring the sides of the foil up like a tent; seal. Place the loaves on a large baking sheet. Bake for 20–25 minutes. Open foil and sprinkle 2 tablespoons Parmesan cheese on each half. Slice each bread half into 2- to 3-inch pieces, about 7 per half.

PER SLICE: 162 calories, 21.5 grams carbohydrate, 3.3 grams fat, 11.4 grams protein.

LEAD PASS:

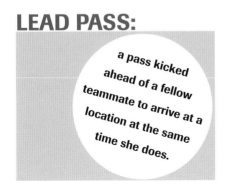

a pass kicked ahead of a fellow teammate to arrive at a location at the same time she does.

"Mismatch" Mixed Squash Bake

SERVES 12

Canola or olive oil
    cooking spray
3 medium zucchini, sliced in
    coins, skin on
3 medium yellow summer
    squash, sliced lengthwise,
    then ¼ inch slices, skin on
3 Roma tomatoes (about
    2 cups), quartered,
    cut into chunks
½ teaspoon basil
¼ teaspoon minced garlic
1 teaspoon salt
Dash pepper
¼ cup shredded sharp
    cheddar cheese
¼ cup grated Parmesan cheese
⅓ cup dry breadcrumbs
½ cup shredded mozzarella
    cheese

Not many carbohydrates, so
increase with other foods such as a
green salad and/or brown rice.

Preheat oven to 350°F. Spray a
2-quart casserole dish with nonstick
cooking spray; set aside. Combine
zucchini, squash, tomatoes,
seasonings, and cheddar. Place
veggie mixture in casserole dish.
Combine the Parmesan and the
breadcrumbs. Sprinkle over veggies.
Bake for about 35 minutes. Remove
from oven and sprinkle with
mozzarella. Bake 10 minutes
longer.

PER ½ CUP SERVING: 62 calories,
 6 grams carbohydrate,
2.5 grams fat, 3.8 grams protein.

MISMATCH:

the situation that occurs when a particular offensive player is far superior to the defender marking (defending) him.

"Stopper" Shrimp and Pasta

SERVES 6

1 teaspoon sesame oil
2 cloves garlic, minced
1 tablespoon white
    cooking wine
½ teaspoon salt
1 pound medium shrimp,
    rinsed, peeled, deveined
1 tablespoon sesame oil
2 cups steamed asparagus, cut
    into 2 inch pieces
6 cups cooked angel hair pasta
Parmesan cheese, optional

Feel free to add more veggies,
if you like.

Combine first 4 ingredients in a
bowl or Ziploc bag. Add shrimp
and marinate about 30 minutes.
Drain shrimp, then sauté in
sesame oil in a heated skillet over
medium heat. Meanwhile, steam
or microwave asparagus until
crisp-tender. Toss with shrimp
and pasta. Serve with shredded
Parmesan, if desired.

PER SERVING (with 1 cup pasta):
362 calories, 42.4 grams
carbohydrate, 7.5 grams fat,
31.3 grams protein.

STOPPER:

the defender
that marks the best
player on the attacking
team, usually the
striker.

"Foul Play " Stuffed Chicken

SERVES 8

Canola or olive oil
   cooking spray
4 boneless, skinless
   chicken breasts,
    cut into bite-size pieces
1 tablespoon olive oil
2 tablespoons minced onion
1 cup chopped celery
1 cup sliced fresh mushrooms
1 ½ teaspoons sage
1 teaspoon poultry seasoning
½ teaspoon salt
¼ teaspoon pepper
10 cups dry bread (mix of
   leftovers such as white,
    whole wheat, rye), cubed
2½ cups chicken broth

Moderate fiber and plenty of carbs for fueling.

Preheat oven to 350°F. Spray a 2- or 3-quart baking dish with nonstick cooking spray. In a skillet over medium high heat, lightly sauté chicken breast pieces in olive oil. Stir in onion, celery, and mushrooms, adding another tablespoon of olive oil, if necessary, and sauté 2–3 minutes longer. Stir in seasonings.

Pour cooked chicken and veggies in a large bowl and toss with bread cubes. Pour enough broth over mixture to moisten. Transfer mixture to prepared baking dish. Cover and bake for about 30 minutes. Remove cover and bake 5–10 minutes more to brown.

PER SERVING: 272 calories, 35.3 grams carbohydrate, 4.3 grams fat, 23.3 grams protein.

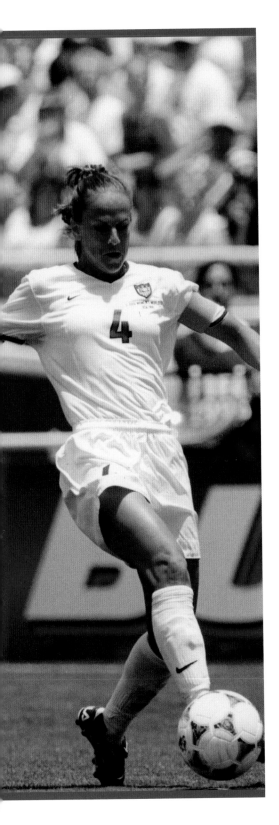

"Assist" Zucchini and Rice Bake

SERVES 4

Canola or olive oil
    cooking spray
1 tablespoon canola margarine
2 medium zucchini, shredded,
    skin included
2 cups cooked rice
¼ cup egg substitute,
    such as Egg Beaters
½ cup shredded Swiss cheese
½ teaspoon salt
Dash pepper

See how that rice zipped the carbs up? That's what I call an assist! Fiber-rich zucchini alone doesn't contribute much in the way of carbs.

Preheat oven to 375°F. Spray a 2-quart casserole dish with nonstick cooking spray. Melt margarine in a skillet over high heat; sauté zucchini about 2 minutes, stirring constantly. Remove from heat; add rice, egg substitute, cheese, salt, and pepper. Pour into dish. Bake for 20 minutes, until heated through and slightly browned.

PER ½ CUP SERVING: 198 calories, 29.1 grams carbohydrate, 4.8 grams fat, 9.4 grams protein.

ASSIST:

the pass or passes made to a player before scoring a goal. Up to two assists can be credited for one goal.

 # Fruitful Refueling: Post-Game Foods

Fuel tanks aren't completely drained when an event is finished, we hope. In any case, this is a critical time to work on refueling. It's crucial to consume carbohydrate-rich foods and beverages within the first 30 minutes, and up to 2 hours, after the event. You should shoot for 150–200 grams. A sample meal might look like so: 1½ cups spaghetti with meat sauce (74 grams), 1 cup broccoli (6 grams), 1 freshly baked "Pop It" Piping Hot Breadstick (34 grams), 1 cup green salad with Italian dressing (11 grams), 8 ounces sparkling juice (40 grams), and ½ cup sorbet (30 grams) for a grand total of 195 grams carbohydrate.

Post-game foods can easily include high-carbohydrate, high-fiber choices such as beans and cabbage, if your child is accustomed to a regular intake of gassy foods such as these. If not, serve these foods after the game so problems don't impact performance.

POST-GAME LUNCHES

"Brilliant" Beef 'n' Bean Bake

SERVES 10

Canola or olive oil cooking spray
2 pounds lean ground beef
    (preferably 93-percent lean)
2 tablespoons red onion, minced
1 can (15 ounces) dark red kidney
    beans, drained, rinsed
1 can (15 ounces) black beans,
    drained, rinsed
1 can (15 ounces) lima beans,
    drained, rinsed
¼ cup molasses
1 cup ketchup
¼ cup stone-ground mustard
1 teaspoon liquid smoke
1 clove garlic, minced
1 teaspoon salt
Dash pepper
¼ cup real bacon bits

Not just your typical baked beans!
Good source of carbs but add more
for optimal refueling.

Preheat oven to 375°F. Spray a
3-quart casserole dish with
nonstick cooking spray. Brown
beef with onion; drain. Place in
casserole dish and add all of the
beans. Gently mix together. In a
separate bowl, combine molasses,
ketchup, mustard, liquid smoke,
garlic, salt, and pepper and pour
over beef and bean mixture and
mix well. Sprinkle bacon bits on
top. Cover and bake for about
1 hour.

PER SERVING: 313 calories,
34.4 grams carbohydrate,
7.5 grams fat, 26.9 grams protein.

"Set Play" Carrot 'n' Fruit Salad

SERVES 10

3 cups shredded carrots
(about 9 ounces)
8 ounces crushed
pineapple, drained
½ cup dark raisins
½ cup golden raisins
¼ cup dried cranberries
¼ cup reduced-fat mayonnaise
¼ cup low-fat vanilla yogurt

Get set to enjoy lots of color and nutrient variety! You can easily decrease the amount of dressing, if you prefer.

Combine the carrots, pineapple, raisins, and cranberries in a large bowl; set aside. Combine the mayonnaise and the yogurt. Mix well then pour over the carrot mixture; toss gently. Chill or serve immediately.

PER ½ CUP SERVING: 121 calories, 24.1 grams carbohydrate, 2.1 grams fat, 1.4 grams protein.

"Counter Attack"
Cherry-Rhubarb and Apple Crisp

SERVES 12

Canola oil cooking spray
10 cups McIntosh apples, peeled,
     sliced into bite-sized chunks
1 cup fresh rhubarb, washed,
     trimmed, sliced into
     1-inch pieces
2 cups tart cherries, pitted
½ cup canola margarine, melted
1½ cups brown sugar, packed
2 cups old-fashioned oats
⅔ cup flour
1 teaspoon cinnamon

A great way to keep the refueling
process going. A tasty fruit and
fiber combo!

Preheat oven to 375°F. Spray a
9-inch x 13-inch baking pan with
nonstick cooking spray. Combine
prepared fruit and spread to cover
across bottom of pan.

Combine margarine, brown sugar,
oats, flour, and cinnamon; mixture
should be crumbly. Sprinkle over
fruit. Bake 30–40 minutes or until
topping is lightly browned.

PER SERVING: 326 calories,
58.8 grams carbohydrate,
8.7 grams fat, 2.9 grams protein.

"Forward Line" Fruity Slaw

SERVES 8

2 Fuji apples, coarsely chopped,
    peel on
1 Granny Smith apple, coarsely
    chopped, peel on
2 cups cabbage, finely shredded
1 cup seedless red grapes,
    cut in ½
½ cup golden raisins
½ cup miniature marshmallows
½ cup pecans, toasted, chopped
1 cup vanilla yogurt
1 tablespoon lemon juice

This is kind of like a Waldorf Salad. Give it a try!

Toss apple with cabbage, grapes, raisins, marshmallows, and pecans. Combine yogurt and lemon juice; pour over mixture and gently toss to coat. Cover and chill.

PER ½ CUP SERVING: 226 calories, 30.7 grams carbohydrate, 10 grams fat, 3.5 grams protein.

"Linea de Fuego" Homemade Salsa

**MAKES ABOUT
1½ QUARTS**

1 can (28 ounces) tomato puree,
    drained with juice reserved
3 green onions (about ⅓ cup),
    cleaned, sliced into pieces,
    greens and tops
½ jalapeño pepper
2 tablespoons fresh cilantro
    leaves (or 2 teaspoons dried)
Dash of garlic powder
1½ teaspoons salt
1 teaspoon balsamic vinegar

A QUICK STAPLE when you're in the "line of fire" to prep a healthy lunch. Great with chips or tortillas, or as a condiment. Adds carbs but very little fat. Very versatile. Careful on the hot spices!

Chill tomato puree. Finely chop onion and pepper in a food processor (or by hand!). Blend in tomatoes; process to desired consistency, adding liquid as necessary. Stir in remaining ingredients and mix well. Serve immediately, but chilling helps blend flavors. Keeps refrigerated for about 1 week.

NOTE: Adjust ingredients such as onion, jalapeno, cilantro, and salt to desired taste.

PER ½ CUP SERVING: 53 calories, 10.1 grams carbohydrate, .4 grams fat, 2.3 grams protein.

"Wingers" Lentil Burritos

SERVES 8

1 cup lentils

2 cups water

½ cup minced onion (or
⅛ teaspoon onion powder)

1 clove garlic, minced

½ teaspoon ground cumin

1 cup homemade salsa
(page 80)

1 cup zucchini, finely chopped

4 ounces shredded
mozzarella cheese

8 flour tortillas (white or
whole wheat)

A good "make and take" food item for those days you're on the run, these are good served warm or cold. Lentils are an excellent source of protein and fiber.

Rinse lentils. Place in a medium saucepan with water, onion, garlic, and cumin. Heat to boiling; cover and reduce heat. Simmer 10–12 minutes, or just until lentils are barely tender. Drain; set aside. Combine salsa, zucchini, and cheese. Spoon about ½ cup lentil mixture down the center of each tortilla; fold into burritos. Serve immediately or warm for 20 seconds in a microwave.

PER BURRITO: 279 Calories, 38.1 grams carbohydrate, 7.7 grams fat, 14.4 grams protein.

WINGERS:

the outside forwards who play to the sides of the strikers. Often they are the team's fastest players, best dribblers, and most accurate passers.

"All-Star" Meat and Potato Loaf

SERVES 10

Canola or olive oil
    cooking spray
1½ pounds lean ground beef
1 cup shredded potatoes
    (fresh, refrigerated, or frozen)
½ cup crushed saltines
    (about 12 squares)
2 tablespoons finely
    minced onion
½ teaspoon salt
⅛ teaspoon pepper
1 clove garlic, minced
½ tablespoon stone-ground
    mustard
⅛ teaspoon ground sage
½ cup low-fat milk
    (1 percent fat)
¼ cup egg substitute, such as
    Egg Beaters
1 teaspoon Worcestershire sauce

TOPPING:

⅓ cup ketchup
1 tablespoon coarse-ground
    mustard
1 tablespoon brown sugar

GREAT SERVED COLD on bread with a little mayo!

Preheat oven to 350°F. Spray a 9-inch x 5-inch loaf pan with nonstick cooking spray. In a large bowl, combine ground beef, potatoes, crushed saltines, onion, and next 5 seasonings; mix well.

In a separate bowl, combine milk, egg, and Worcestershire sauce; beat to blend. Stir into meat mixture and knead to thoroughly combine ingredients. Place meat in baking pan and shape to form 1 large loaf. Combine topping ingredients. Whisk to blend. Pour over meatloaf. Bake 1–1½ hours, until browned.

PER SERVING: 137 calories, 7.1 grams carbohydrate, 5.4 grams fat, 15 grams protein.

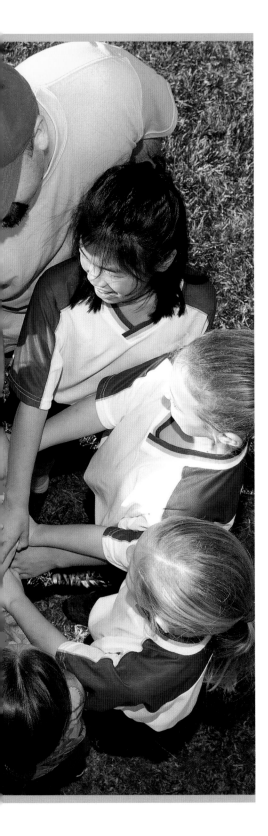

"Smooth Pace" Peach Smoothie

SERVES 6

6 ounces orange-peach-mango
   juice concentrate, thawed
1 cup water
1 cup low-fat milk
   (1 percent fat)
1 cup canned sliced peaches,
   juice pack, drained
   (or 1 cup sliced mango)
2 tablespoons sugar
1 teaspoon vanilla
Crushed ice

Use fresh peaches, if available!

Combine first 6 ingredients in a blender. Process until smooth. Add crushed ice to 6-cup level; blend until smooth. Serve immediately.

PER SERVING: 112 calories, 24.9 grams carbohydrate, 0.4 grams fat, 2.1 grams protein.

"Power Up" Pork and Pinto Burritos

SERVES 8

2½ pounds lean, boneless
    pork loin roast, trimmed
    of excess fat
1 pound dried pinto beans
½ teaspoon ground cumin
1 tablespoon salt
2 cloves garlic, minced
¼ teaspoon oregano leaves
8 flour tortillas

OPTIONAL TOPPINGS:

Shredded cheese such
    as Colby Jack
Salsa
Chopped tomatoes
Chopped green onion
Low-fat sour cream
Guacamole

Build as you like it!

Place roast in a slow cooker. Sort and wash beans. Pour on top of roast. Add seasonings. Pour water, 2–3 quarts, over all ingredients to cover. Cover with lid and cook on low 6–8 hours, stirring occasionally and adding water as needed (do not let beans dry out). Once beans are cooked, remove roast to a cutting board. Let sit about 5 minutes, then flake with a fork into chunks, and place back in pot.

TO ASSEMBLE BURRITOS:

With slotted spoon, place bean/meat mixture down center of tortilla. Add optional toppings such as 2 tablespoons shredded cheese (can go inside and/or outside tortilla, depending on personal preference). Microwave 20 seconds to melt cheese. Roll like a burrito and add additional toppings as desired, such as 1 tablespoon low-fat sour cream spread across top, with 1–2 tablespoons salsa, and 1 tablespoon cheese.

PER BURRITO (with cheese, sour cream, and salsa, as above): 340 calories, 38.2 grams carbohydrate, 9.9 grams fat, 24.5 grams protein.

"Running Hard" Rice 'n' Noodles

SERVES 4

1 tablespoon canola margarine
1 cup long grain rice, uncooked
½ cup fine egg noodles,
    uncooked
2¾ cups chicken broth
    (22 ounces)

Kind of like Rice-A-Roni. Try using wild rice to increase the fiber.

Melt the margarine over high heat in a skillet. Add the rice and noodles; sauté, stirring constantly until lightly browned, about 2 minutes. Stir in the chicken broth and bring the mixture to a boil. Reduce heat; cover, and simmer for 20–25 minutes or until broth is absorbed and rice is tender.

PER SERVING: 259 calories, 41.6 grams carbohydrate, 5.2 grams fat, 11.6 grams protein.

"Shielding" Southwestern Salad

SERVES 8

2 cups mixed salad greens, torn
1 cup iceberg lettuce, torn
1 cup fresh spinach leaves,
    stemmed, torn
1 can (15 ounces) dark red
    kidney beans, drained, rinsed
1 can (15 ounces) black beans,
    drained, rinsed
¼ teaspoon onion powder
¼ teaspoon garlic powder
¼ cup salsa, such as "Linea de
    Fuego" (page 80)
¾ cup shredded Colby
    Jack cheese
¾ cup shredded
    mozzarella cheese
¼ cup shredded sharp
    cheddar cheese
2 cups Roma tomatoes,
    quartered, cut into chunks
¼ cup sliced green onion
Salsa
Tortilla chips

Enjoy with a moderate serving of tortilla chips, if desired.

Mix salad greens together and place in a 9-inch x 13-inch dish. Combine beans, onion and garlic powders, and ¼ cup salsa. Pour evenly over salad greens. Combine cheeses and sprinkle over salad. Sprinkle tomato and green onion over all. Serve with more salsa and tortilla chips.

PER SERVING: 222 calories, 24.7 grams carbohydrate, 7.2 grams fat, 15 grams protein.

SHIELDING:

a technique used by a ball carrier to protect the ball from a defender closely marking him.

"Varsity" Veggie Sandwich

SERVES 1

2 slices whole-wheat bread
¼ cup hummus (either
    store-bought or "Home
    Team" Hummus on page 133)
1 tablespoon low-fat
    cream cheese
¼ cucumber, thinly sliced
1 carrot, coarsely grated

Add a handful of carrot sticks, a small bunch of grapes, and a glass of milk for a primo after-workout lunch.

Spread 1 piece of bread with the hummus; spread the other piece with cream cheese. Lay out cucumber slices evenly over the hummus, then top with grated carrot. Place bread with cream cheese on top of the veggie layers and press gently but firmly.

PER SERVING: 279 calories,
38.4 grams carbohydrate,
11.1 grams fat, 11.6 grams protein.

"Spring League" Soba Noodle Salad

SERVES 2

8 ounces green beans, trimmed
   cut into 2-inch pieces
1 medium carrot,
   diagonally sliced
6 ounces buckwheat soba
   noodles (or pasta
   such as linguine)
6 ounces firm silken tofu, cubed
3 tablespoons fresh lime juice
2 tablespoons soy sauce
2 teaspoons toasted sesame oil
2 green onions, minced
½ cup canned mushrooms,
   drained

If "tofu" is a scary word in your house, this recipe may allay some of those fears. Let your kids try eating it with chopsticks for fun, and to slow ingestion by ravenous kids, who sometimes eat too fast for healthy digestion.

In a large pot of boiling water, cook the green beans and the carrots until crisp-tender, about 4 minutes. Transfer veggies to colander to drain and set aside. In the same pot, cook the noodles according to their package instructions; drain but do not rinse.

Place tofu cubes in a bowl. In another bowl, whisk lime juice, soy sauce, and sesame oil. Pour half of the dressing over the tofu and toss gently to coat.

In a large bowl, toss the noodles, green beans, carrots, green onions, and mushrooms with the remaining dressing. Sprinkle tofu on top. Let cool and serve.

PER SERVING: 479 calories, 88.5 grams carbohydrate, 7.6 grams fat, 24 grams protein.

"Top-Drawer" Tostada

SERVES 4

1 can (16 ounces) fat-free
   refried beans
4 whole wheat tortillas
½ cup chopped red onion
½ cup shredded romaine lettuce
½ cup shredded red cabbage
½ cup chopped green
   bell pepper
½ cup chopped tomatoes
½ cup grated cheddar cheese
Low-fat sour cream
Salsa

Pile on the veggies! This is really a yummy, super-easy, and nutrient-packed lunch.

In a saucepan over medium heat, cook the beans for 3–4 minutes until heated through. Heat a large non-stick skillet over high heat. Heat tortillas, one at a time, 1–2 minutes on each side.

Spread ½ cup beans on each tortilla. Over the beans, layer onion, lettuce, cabbage, bell pepper, tomatoes, and cheddar. Serve with a dollop of sour cream and salsa to taste.

PER SERVING: 448 calories, 70.5 grams carbohydrate, 9 grams fat, 19 grams protein.

"Sandwiched" Ham, Cheese & Pineapple

SERVES 4

3 tablespoons butter or
  margarine, softened
8 slices bread
4 slices Swiss cheese
8 slices cooked ham,
  thinly sliced
Fresh pineapple, thinly sliced
  into 8 rounds

Grilled ham and cheese with pineapple. Aloha! This sandwich isn't illegal; it's just tropical. Add a fruit salad to further boost the carbs.

Heat a large skillet over medium-high heat. Spread butter onto 1 side of each slice of bread. Place as many as 4 slices of bread, butter side down in the skillet. Top each with 1 slice of cheese, 2 slices of ham, and 2 pineapple rounds. Place remaining slices of bread on top with the butter side up. When the bottom of the sandwich is golden brown, 2–3 minutes, flip sandwiches, and cook until browned on the other side and cheese is melted, about 1 minute.

Repeat steps with remaining ingredients, if all 4 sandwiches do not fit in the skillet.

PER SERVING: 499 calories, 32.2 grams carbohydrate, 28.2 grams fat, 27.9 grams protein.

SANDWICH: an illegal act of obstruction is which two players from one team impede the movement of a player from the other team with contact from two different sides at the same time.

"YHTBT" Wraps

SERVES 2

1 cup hummus (either
    store-bought or "Home
    Team" Hummus on page 133)
2 sandwich wraps (or
    12-inch tortillas)
1 cup grated carrots
1 Granny Smith apple,
    sliced thinly
½ cup baby spinach (about
    1 packed cup)
½ cup herb salad or baby
    greens mix

These hummus wraps are hard to explain. You have to taste them to understand how good they are.

Spread ½ cup hummus on each wrap, leaving a 2-inch border. Arranging ingredients in the center of each, layer wraps with ½ cup grated carrot, half of the sliced apple, and half of the greens.

Fold in sides about 1 inch, then roll firmly from one of the open ends. Cut rolled wraps in half diagonally.

PER SERVING: 526 calories,
89.5 grams carbohydrate,
12.9 grams fat, 15.9 grams protein.

YHTBT:

stands for "you had to be there," as in, "I can't explain how it felt to win the Gold. You had to be there."

POST-GAME DINNERS
"Set Play" Sweet Potato

SERVES 1

1 sweet potato (4 ounces), skin on,
  cleaned, pricked
1 teaspoon canola margarine
Salt and pepper, to taste

LOOK AT THAT CARB count! More than a russet! Enjoy all by itself. But it makes a great "bowl" for chili, too.

Preheat oven to 400°F. Wrap potato in foil and bake 45 minutes to 1 hour. Poke with a fork to check for tenderness. After baking, remove foil and slice the potato down the middle. Fluff the inside and mix with margarine. Season to taste.

PER SERVING: 152 calories, 27.5 grams carbohydrate, 3.8 grams fat, 2 grams protein.

SET PLAY:

a planned strategy that a team uses when a game is restarted with a free kick, penalty kick, corner kick, goal kick, throw-in, or kickoff.

Chunky Cran-Apple Sauce

SERVES 6

8–10 large Granny Smith apples,
    peeled, cut into chunks
½ cup dried cranberries
½ cup brown sugar
⅔ cup water
½ teaspoon ground cinnamon

JUST LIKE GRANDMA used to make! Although, she probably used raw cranberries. (Note: Dried cranberries are a good food to have on hand when you're on the run.)

Combine apples, cranberries, brown sugar, water, and cinnamon in a 2- to 3-quart saucepan with lid. Simmer over low heat for 15–20 minutes. Remove from heat. Mash to desired consistency or leave as is. Chill.

PER ½ CUP SERVING: 98 calories, 24 grams carbohydrate, 0.2 grams fat, 0.1 grams protein.

CHUNKING:

the awareness of other players' existence and positions; vision.

"Cheeky" Cheesy Meatballs

SERVES 8-16

Canola or olive oil
   cooking spray
3 pounds lean ground beef
   (preferably 93 percent lean)
2 tablespoons chopped onion
2 cups dry breadcrumbs
¼ cup egg substitute, such as
   Egg Beaters
⅓ cup low-fat milk (1 percent fat)
1 teaspoon salt
Pepper to taste
½ teaspoon garlic powder
1 package (8 ounce) Monterey
   Jack cheese, cut into 16 cubes
Flour
Olive oil
1 jar (14 ounces) pizza sauce

Higher fat and calories, but better now than just before a game. These make a nice accompaniment to pasta or rice.

Preheat oven to 375°F. Spray a 9-inch x 13-inch baking pan with nonstick cooking spray; set aside.

Combine ground beef, onion, breadcrumbs, egg substitute, milk, and seasonings in a bowl. Knead to blend thoroughly. Divide into 16 portions of about ⅓ cup each. Form a meaty ball around each piece of cheese, covering cheese completely. Roll balls in flour.

Heat 1 tablespoon of olive oil in a skillet over medium high heat. Brown meatballs, turning constantly and not cooking so long that cheese begins oozing out.

Place browned meatballs into the prepared baking pan and pour sauce over all the balls. Bake for about 35 minutes.

PER MEATBALL: 274 calories, 16.7 grams carbohydrate, 12.9 grams fat, 22.8 grams protein.

"Down the Line" Dilly Potato Salad

SERVES 12

3 pounds red potatoes, rinsed,
  cut in ½, peel left on

¼ cup plain yogurt

¼ cup reduced-fat mayonnaise

2 tablespoons balsamic vinegar

2 tablespoons stone-
  ground mustard

1 tablespoon dill relish

1 teaspoon salt

1 teaspoon fresh dill

3 hard-cooked eggs,
  peeled, chopped

Paprika

ADD A LEAN hamburger with cheese to the plate, then some fruit, or a smoothie!

Bring about 3 quarts of water to a boil. Add the potatoes and cook until tender. Drain and cool; when cool, cut potatoes into cubes.

In the meantime, combine yogurt, mayonnaise, vinegar, mustard, relish, salt, and dill; chill. Place potato cubes in a large bowl. Gently stir in eggs. Pour chilled dressing over mixture and toss to coat; garnish lightly with paprika. Chill and serve.

PER ½ CUP SERVING: 130 calories, 21.4 grams carbohydrate, 3.1 grams fat, 4.1 grams protein.

"Pop It" Piping Hot Breadsticks

MAKES 12 BREADSTICKS

Canola or olive oil
   cooking spray
12 frozen dinner rolls, thawed
Olive oil

TOPPINGS (per breadstick):
1 tablespoon Parmesan
   cheese, optional
¼ teaspoon minced garlic
¼ teaspoon toasted sesame seeds

Regardless of what the "Atkins" people say, your kids need some bread. These are best when served straight from the oven.

Preheat oven to 350°F. Spray a baking sheet with nonstick cooking spray; set aside.

Lightly flour a cutting board and roll each dinner roll to a length of about 6 inches. Lightly brush top with olive oil. Sprinkle with all toppings or customize according to personal preference.

Place each breadstick on baking sheet, at least 2 inches apart. Bake 10–15 minutes or until golden brown.

PER BREADSTICK: 157calories, 27 grams carbohydrate, 3.1 grams fat, 5.2 grams protein.

POP IT:

to pass it to oneself.

"Gold Medal" Lasagna

SERVES 12

Canola or olive oil
   cooking spray
1 pound lean ground beef
   (preferably 93 percent lean)
2 tablespoons minced onion
1 clove garlic
1 can (29 ounces) tomato sauce
6 ounces tomato paste
½ cup water
2 tablespoons red cooking wine
1 teaspoon basil
½ teaspoon oregano
½ cup egg substitute, such as
   Egg Beaters
15 ounces low-fat ricotta cheese
¾ cup grated Parmesan
   cheese, divided
1 teaspoon salt
½ teaspoon pepper
8 oven-ready lasagna
   noodles, dry
½ pound low-fat mozzarella
   cheese (2 cups), shredded

A true favorite around the world.

Preheat oven to 350°F. Spray a 9-inch x 13-inch baking pan with nonstick cooking spray.

In a skillet, brown ground beef, onion, and garlic; drain and set aside.

Combine tomato sauce, tomato paste, water, wine, basil, and oregano; simmer 15 minutes, stirring occasionally. In a separate bowl, combine egg substitute, ricotta cheese, ½ cup of the Parmesan, salt, and pepper. Cover bottom of baking pan with half of the meat sauce. Layer with 4 noodles, slightly overlapping sheets (see package instructions), half ricotta mixture, and 1 cup mozzarella cheese. Repeat, beginning with meat sauce and ending with mozzarella cheese. Cover with foil and bake for 40 minutes.

Remove foil, sprinkle with 1/4 cup Parmesan cheese and bake an additional 10 minutes. Let sit about 15 minutes before cutting into 12 pieces.

PER SERVING: 249 calories, 18.4 grams carbohydrate, 9.6 grams fat, 22.1 grams protein.

"Numbers Up" Noodles and Steak Parmesan

SERVES 6

1¼ pounds tenderized
    round steak

2 tablespoons flour

½ cup dry breadcrumbs

½ teaspoon garlic powder

½ cup Parmesan cheese, grated

½ cup egg substitute, such
    as Egg Beaters

2 tablespoons water

Olive oil

Canola or olive oil
    cooking spray

1 can (6 ounces) tomato paste

2 cups water

¼ teaspoon onion powder

½ teaspoon sugar

½ teaspoon marjoram

½ teaspoon salt

Dash pepper

1½ cups shredded
    mozzarella cheese

6 cups thin egg noodles,
    cooked (may prep while
    meat is cooked)

"Expensive" in calories but worth it at a time your kids can most afford it . . . like post game.

Preheat oven to 350°F. Trim meat of excess fat and cut into 6–8 equal pieces; set aside.

Combine flour, breadcrumbs, garlic powder, and Parmesan cheese in a Ziploc bag. In a separate bowl, combine egg substitute and water. First, dip meat in egg substitute mix, then place each piece in the Ziploc with the breadcrumb mixture and shake to coat.

Heat 2 tablespoons oil in a skillet over medium high heat. Lightly brown each side of meat in skillet after coating. Remove from skillet and place in a 9-inch x 13-inch baking dish sprayed with nonstick cooking spray.

Combine tomato paste, water, onion powder, sugar, marjoram, salt, and pepper in a 2-quart saucepan. Bring to a boil then reduce to a simmer for 5 minutes, stirring constantly. Pour two-thirds of the sauce over meat. Sprinkle with mozzarella cheese; top with remaining sauce. Cover with foil. Bake for about 1 hour. Serve with 1 cup noodles, prepared as directed on package. This dish can easily be left in the oven at a low temperature after the initial hour of baking. Nice and tender!

PER SERVING: 421 calories, 41.9 grams carbohydrate, 34 grams fat, 13.1 grams protein.

NUMBERS UP: *a numerical advantage.*

"Power Kick" Pork Chili with Beans

SERVES 10

1 tablespoon canola oil
2 pounds lean boneless pork
    roast, cut into 1-inch cubes
1 clove garlic, minced
2 tablespoons minced onion
1 can (15 ounces) dark red
    kidney beans, drained, rinsed
1 can (15 ounces) black beans,
    drained, rinsed
1 can (29 ounces)
    crushed tomatoes
2 cups water
1 teaspoon beef
    bouillon granules
½ teaspoon cumin

Not your typical chili. Serve with "Corner Kick" Corny Whole-Grain Muffins (on page 102) for even more carbs.

Heat oil in a stockpot over medium high heat. Cook pork cubes with garlic and onion until lightly browned. Add the beans, tomatoes, water, bouillon, and cumin. Bring to a boil. Reduce heat to low, cover and simmer 2 hours, or until meat is tender.

PER SERVING: 261 calories, 22.9 grams carbohydrate, 6.7 grams fat, 27.1 grams protein.

"Pitch Perfect" Split Pea Soup

SERVES 8

1 pound green split peas
   (2¼ cups), uncooked
2 tablespoons minced onion
¼ teaspoon dried marjoram
1 cup peeled, cubed
   red potatoes
1 cup diced celery
1 cup baby carrots, cut
   diagonally in half
1 teaspoon salt
Dash pepper
½ teaspoon liquid smoke

Healthy—and green (like the pitch)! Ask your split-pea-rebellious kids to close their eyes and give it a try.

Cover peas with 2 quarts cold water in a large stock pot; simmer gently 2 minutes. Remove from heat; cover and let stand 1 hour. Add onion, marjoram, vegetables, salt, pepper, and liquid smoke. Bring to a boil; reduce heat and simmer 30–40 minutes (if variation is used, add meat at this time).

VARIATION: Add 1 cup cubed, lean ham.

PER SERVING: 225 calories, 39.9 grams carbohydrate, 0.8 grams fat, 14.6 grams protein.

PITCH:

the term used to describe the playing field.

"Wingback" Wacky White Chili

SERVES 8

1 pound great Northern
    beans, dry
6 cups chicken broth
2 cloves garlic, minced
1 tablespoon chopped onions,
    divided
½ tablespoon olive oil
4 boneless, skinless chicken
    breasts, cut into pieces
1 teaspoon ground cumin
1 teaspoon oregano leaves
2 teaspoons salt
⅛–¼ teaspoon cayenne pepper
Salsa, optional
Cheddar cheese, shredded,
    optional
Jalapeños, sliced, optional

Great in a bowl, but some wrap it in a tortilla like a burrito . . . just more carbs that way. It's also a tasty baked potato topper with chives and a sprinkle of grated cheddar.

Rinse and sort beans. Combine beans, chicken broth, garlic, and onion in a large stock pot. Bring to a boil and simmer until very soft (2½–3 hours); may need to add more broth.

Meanwhile, place oil in a skillet over high heat. Add chicken and sauté until cooked through; add water if extra liquid is needed. Sprinkle seasonings atop and mix well. Remove from heat. Stir chicken into bean mixture once beans are cooked. Simmer about 30 minutes more. If you like, serve with salsa, shredded cheese, and/or sliced jalapeños.

SLOW COOKER VARIATION: Place beans, broth, garlic, and onions in a slow cooker; add additional broth as needed. Prepare the seasoned chicken and store in the fridge until ready to add. Once beans are cooked, add the chicken mixture and simmer 30 minutes more.

PER SERVING: 322 calories, 37.1 grams carbohydrate, 4.1 grams fat, 33.8 grams protein.

WINGBACK:

a fullback playing on the outside, with the task of making attacking plays by coming forward, usually by overlapping.

"Corner Kick" Corny Whole-Grain Muffins

SERVES 8

Canola oil cooking spray
  (or 8 muffin cup liners)
½ cup flour
½ cup whole wheat flour
¾ cup cornmeal
3 tablespoons sugar
2½ teaspoons baking powder
1 teaspoon salt
⅓ cup egg substitute, such
  as Egg Beaters
1 cup low-fat milk
  (1 percent fat)
2 tablespoons canola oil

Adds a little more fiber than most cornbread.

Preheat oven to 400°F. Spray the bottom of 8 muffin cups (or use liners); set aside. Combine flours, cornmeal, sugar, baking powder, and salt in a bowl. Whisk to blend. In a measuring cup, combine egg substitute, milk, and oil; stir into the dry ingredients just until moistened. Fill muffin cups two-thirds full. Bake for 15–18 minutes, until golden brown or toothpick inserted in the center of a muffin comes out clean.

PER MUFFIN: 172 calories,
28.1 grams carbohydrate,
4.2 grams fat, 5.1 grams protein.

"Karaoke" Broken Pasta With Peanut Sauce

SERVES 4

3 tablespoons soy sauce

3 tablespoons rice vinegar

2 tablespoons smooth
   peanut butter

1 tablespoon honey

1 ½ teaspoons minced
   garlic from jar

2 tablespoons minced
   fresh ginger

2 eggplants, peeled, cubed

8 ounces snow peas, sliced in
   half diagonally

2 red bell peppers, cut into
   ½-inch-wide strips

8 ounces lasagna noodles,
   broken into large pieces

2 tablespoons roasted
   peanuts, crushed

This Asian-style pasta dish sings with fresh veggies in a sweet, nutty sauce.

In a large bowl, whisk together soy sauce, vinegar, peanut butter, honey, garlic, and ginger. Set aside.

Steam eggplants in a steaming basket until tender, about 15 minutes. Add snow peas and bell peppers; cook until crisp-tender and until eggplant is tender, about 5 minutes.

While vegetables steam, cook pasta in salted boiling water until al dente, according to the package instructions. Drain.

Add pasta and veggies to set-aside bowl of soy-peanut sauce. Toss to coat. Sprinkle with crushed peanuts.

PER SERVING: 369 calories, 68.9 grams carbohydrate, 5.4 grams fat, 14.1 grams protein.

KARAOKE:

moving sideways quickly by crossing over one's legs.

"Take On" Tacos

SERVES 4

2 tablespoons olive oil
1 medium onion, finely chopped
2 teaspoons minced garlic
    from jar
1 jalapeño, minced, ribs
    and seeds removed
2 cans (15.5 ounces each)
    black-eyed peas,
    drained, rinsed
10 ounces corn
2 cups water
½ cup chopped cilantro
12 corn tortillas, warmed
4 ounces feta cheese
Salsa
Lettuce, shredded, optional
Cabbage, shredded, optional

Black-eyed peas are not just good luck at New Year's. They're also tasty in these tacos, which deliver a fine supply of all three nutrients: carbs, protein, and fat.

Heat oil in a large skillet over medium heat. Sauté onion, garlic, and jalapeño in the skillet until tender, about 5–7 minutes.

Stir in black-eyed peas, corn, and water. Simmer over medium-high heat until corn is tender and liquid has mostly evaporated, about 12–15 minutes. Mix in cilantro and remove from heat.

Fill warmed tortillas with cooked filling, feta, salsa, lettuce, cabbage, and/or your favorite taco garnishes.

PER SERVING: 605 calories, 100.5 grams carbohydrate, 16.4 grams fat, 19.6 grams protein.

TAKE ON:

to challenge a defender while dribbling with the ball.

"Fair Play" Barley Pilaf

SERVES 4

Olive oil cooking spray
8 ounces mushrooms, sliced
1 medium zucchini, chopped
1 medium onion, chopped
½ teaspoon dried oregano
1 cup pearl barley
2 cups chicken broth

This is a quick and easy alternative side dish to rice or pasta. It is high in carbs and fiber, and provides veggies and grains in one yummy dish.

Preheat oven to 350°F. Spray a medium skillet with cooking spray; over medium heat, sauté mushrooms, zucchini, onion, and oregano for 5 minutes.

Add barley and broth to skillet, increase the heat, and bring to a rapid boil.

Into a 2-quart baking dish sprayed with olive oil, transfer all the ingredients and stir well. Cover and bake in oven for about 30 minutes. Check at intervals to add water, if needed.

PER SERVING: 224 calories, 46 grams carbohydrate, 2 grams fat, 8 grams protein.

"Overlap" Greek Omelet

SERVES 2

Olive oil cooking spray
½ cup chopped onion
¾ cup chopped ripe tomato
4 egg whites
2 whole eggs
2 teaspoons water
Salt and pepper to taste
1 tablespoon sliced black olives
4 teaspoons crumbled
   feta cheese

Breakfast for dinner. Why not? Plus, omelets are so easy and can accommodate a variety of tastes and available ingredients. Add a salad and bread to complete the meal.

Preheat nonstick skillet sprayed with olive oil. Add onion to skillet and sauté until tender. Add tomato and cook another 2–3 minutes. Set vegetables aside and keep warm.

Whisk together eggs, water, salt, and pepper.

Respray skillet and pour in beaten egg mixture. Let set slightly. With a heatproof flexible spatula, push eggs from edge toward center. Maneuver pan so egg fills spaces. Repeat until eggs are just set.

Place sautéed vegetables, olives, and feta over half the omelet, leaving the half closer to the skillet handle uncovered. Using the spatula, gently fold omelet over the filling. Cook for another 1–2 minutes, and then slide from pan onto a plate.

Some other filling options:
- Southwestern-style, with pepper Jack cheese, cilantro, and salsa.
- Western, with bacon and cheddar.
- Ham, bell pepper, and green onion.
- Sautéed leftover veggies and Parmesan cheese.

PER SERVING: 169.5 calories, 8.5 grams carbohydrate, 8.5 grams fat, 11.6 grams protein.

OVERLAP:

when a player comes from behind and gets in front of a player (generally with the ball) from his/her own team.

"Coin Tossed" BLT

SERVES 4

8 strips bacon, precooked
    or prepared per
    package instructions
⅓ cup buttermilk
3 tablespoons reduced-fat
    mayonnaise
2 tablespoons cider vinegar
1 green onion, thinly sliced
⅛ teaspoon ground black
    pepper
Salt, to taste
1 head romaine lettuce,
    shredded
1 pint cherry tomatoes, halved
2 cups seasoned croutons

You'll be re-revving engines when you serve this bacon, lettuce, and tomato salad with breadsticks, fruit, and a parfait dessert.

Cook bacon according to package instructions. Drain, crumble, and set aside.

In a large bowl, whisk together buttermilk, mayonnaise, vinegar, onion, and black pepper. Season with salt.

Combine lettuce, tomatoes, and croutons in a large salad bowl. Toss with dressing, sprinkle with bacon, and serve immediately.

PER SERVING: 355 calories, 38.4 grams carbohydrate, 17.9 grams fat, 11.9 grams protein.

COIN TOSS:

a method used by the referee to determine which team kicks off as well as the respective directions of the two teams.

"Smack It" Jacket Potatoes with Ham & Swiss Cheese

SERVES 4

4 baking potatoes (about
   8 ounces each)
1 teaspoon minced garlic
   from jar
2 teaspoons butter
½ cup fat-free milk
½ cup shredded Swiss cheese
½ cup cooked, chopped ham
1 tablespoon chopped
   fresh parsley
Salt and black pepper, to taste

Alongside green beans and garlic bread, these stuffed and baked spuds make a filling and complete dinner.

Preheat oven to 500°F.

Make vent holes in the potatoes with a fork, and place in a circle on paper towels in the microwave. Cover potatoes with wet paper towels. Microwave on high for 12 minutes or until done, rearranging the potatoes halfway through. Let stand 2 minutes, then split, and scoop out the pulp of each, leaving about ¼-inch-thick jacket skins. Reserve jackets; set pulp aside.

Sauté garlic in butter for 30 seconds over medium-high heat. Add milk and bring to simmer. Pour milk mixture over potato pulp. Stir in ¼ cup cheese, ham and parsley, and season with salt and pepper. Mix well. Stuff each jacket with potato mixture and sprinkle evenly with remaining cheese. Bake 8 minutes or until cheese browns.

PER SERVING: 358 calories, 59.8 grams carbohydrate, 7.5 grams fat, 14.1 grams protein.

SMACK IT AWAY:

a crisp redirection of the ball, generally by a defensive player, in order to get it out of the penalty area.

Fun Foods: Snack Ideas

At one time, many well-meaning adults fed kids "quick energy" snacks prior to sports activities. Apparently understanding that carbohydrate was the preferred fuel source for energy, they thought snacks such as candy and soda pop were an optimal choice. Unfortunately, this form of a simple carbohydrate didn't provide the longer-lasting energy needed. Although calorie density was high, nutrient density was sacrificed as many of these types of foods offer calories aplenty but minimal nutrient value, hence the expression "empty calories."

Dole out pre-game snacks as late as 1–2 hours prior to the event. These should be foods that are small in quantity, are easily digestible, and contain about 20–50 grams carbohydrate. Having snacks available during the event, as well as immediately afterward, is helpful, not only to refresh tired and hungry players but also to begin replenishing their glycogen stores. While water does not contribute any calories whatsoever, it is important—very important. Encourage athletes to consistently hydrate themselves with water or even carb-containing beverages, such as Gatorade or Powerade. Avoid offering heavily concentrated fruit juice or carbonated beverages.

PRE-GAME SNACKS
"Banner" Banana Bread

MAKES 2 LOAVES

Canola oil cooking spray
⅓ cup canola margarine
1 cup sugar
2 eggs
3 medium ripe bananas, mashed
½ teaspoon vanilla
1 cup all-purpose flour
1 cup whole wheat flour
1 teaspoon baking soda
1 teaspoon salt

THIS IS TASTY, it packs a little more fiber than most banana breads, and it contributes potassium.

Preheat oven to 350°F. Spray 2 loaf pans (7⅜-inch x 3⅝-inch) with nonstick cooking spray, then lightly flour bottoms; set aside. Cream margarine and sugar; beat in eggs. Stir in bananas and vanilla; mix just until blended. In a separate bowl, combine dry ingredients; gradually stir into banana mixture. Do not over-mix. Divide batter and pour into the 2 loaf pans. Bake for 40–45 minutes. Cool in pans for 10 minutes, then remove to cooling rack.

PER SLICE: 130 calories,
22.3 grams carbohydrate,
3.6 grams fat, 2.1 grams protein.

"Bonzai" Blueberry Muffins

SERVES 12

Canola oil cooking spray
   (or 12 muffin cup liners)
1 cup flour
1 cup whole wheat flour
½ cup sugar
1 tablespoon baking powder
½ teaspoon salt
1½ cups fresh blueberries
   (or frozen)
½ cup canola margarine, melted
½ cup low-fat milk (1 percent fat)
2 eggs, beaten
½ teaspoon vanilla

Muffins like these kick in just the right amount of pre-game carbs.

Preheat oven to 425°F. Prepare 12-cup muffin tin by spraying bottoms with nonstick cooking spray (or use paper liners). Combine flours, sugar, baking powder, and salt in a medium-size bowl. In a separate bowl, toss 1 tablespoon of the flour mixture with the blueberries; set aside. Combine margarine, milk, eggs, and vanilla. Add to dry mixture, stirring just until moistened. Gently stir in blueberries. Fill muffin cups two-thirds full. Bake 15–20 minutes.

PER MUFFIN: 203 calories, 26.9 grams carbohydrate, 8.8 grams fat, 3.9 grams protein.

"Top Roll" Tropical Fresh Fruit Cup

SERVES 12

1 cup cubed fresh pineapple

1 cup cubed cantaloupe

1 cup cubed honeydew

1 cup seedless red grapes

1 cup seedless green grapes

1 cup fresh blueberries

3 kiwifruit, peeled, cut
   into chunks

LIGHT BUT REFRESHING and full of many nutrients.

Combine, chill, and serve. Best the first day.

PER ½ CUP SERVING: 61 calories, 13.9 grams carbohydrate, 0.4 grams fat, 0.8 grams protein.

TOP ROLL (or spin):

forward spin of a ball, tending to keep it on or near the ground.

"Threepeat" Fruit and Cheese Kabobs

SERVES 16

8 ounces mozzarella cheese,
  cut into ½ ounce cubes
8 ounces cheddar cheese,
  cut into ½ ounce cubes
3 apples, cut into bite-size
  cubes, skin on (dipped in
  lemon juice)
3 oranges, peeled, sectioned,
  with each section halved
1 cup red grapes
1 cup green grapes
Long, frilly toothpicks (6-inch)

A mix of all 3 nutrients—carbohydrate, fat, protein. Especially good for those that didn't get to eat prior to the game.

On each toothpick, place 1 cube of each cheese, apple cube, orange section, red grape, and green grape. These are labor-intensive but fun for kids to do; keep an eye on the toothpicks during assembly and out on the playing field!

PER KABOB: 126 calories, 8.8 grams carbohydrate, 6.9 grams fat, 7.4 grams protein.

"Nutmeg" Whole Wheat Pumpkin Bread

MAKES 2 LOAVES

Canola oil cooking spray
½ cup canola oil
1¼ cups sugar
1 egg
1 cup pumpkin
⅓ cup water
1 cup all-purpose flour
¾ cup whole wheat flour
1 teaspoon baking soda
¾ teaspoon salt
½ teaspoon cinnamon
½ teaspoon nutmeg

An old family recipe, once loaded with vegetable oil and sugar. We modified both, and replaced some of the white flour with whole wheat to improve the fiber content. Plus, pumpkin is a great source of vitamin A. This bread has proven to be a hit with kids, and not just at Halloween!

Preheat oven to 350°F. Spray bottoms of 2 loaf pans (7⅜-inch x 3⅝-inch); set aside. Cream oil and sugar; add egg and mix well. At low speed, gradually stir in pumpkin and water. Combine remaining dry ingredients in a separate bowl; then gradually add to pumpkin mixture on low speed. Mix until blended. Divide batter and pour into the 2 pans. Bake for 40–45 minutes, or until golden brown and a cake tester inserted into the middle comes out clean. Cool in pans for 10 minutes, then remove to cooling rack.

PER SLICE: 147 calories, 21.6 grams carbohydrate, 6.1 grams fat, 1.6 grams protein.

NUTMEG:

to pass the ball through the legs of a defender or goalkeeper.

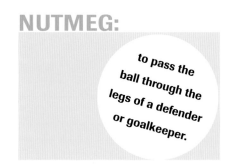

"Kickoff" Apricot-Carrot Muffins with Cornflakes

MAKES 12

8 dried apricots
2 medium carrots
2 eggs or equivalent
  egg substitute
¼ cup honey
2 tablespoons raisins
½ cup chopped almonds
Grated zest from ½ orange
1 cup whole wheat flour
2 teaspoons baking powder
Oil for the muffin pans
2 tablespoons apricot jam
2 tablespoons water
⅓ cup corn flakes

These are an ideal snack-sized source of pre-game carb-loading.

Preheat oven to 400°F. Thinly slice apricots into strips. Grate the peeled carrots and mix with the eggs and honey. Stir in raisins, apricot strips, almonds, and orange zest.

Sift together flour and baking powder, then sift the flour into the apricot mixture, and stir until a stiff batter forms.

Lightly oil the muffin pans and spoon in the batter to no more than two-thirds capacity, as the batter will rise during baking. Smooth the tops. Bake in the middle of the preheated oven for about 20 minutes, until tops are golden brown.

While the muffins are baking, mix together in a small pot the apricot jam and water and warm slowly until fluid-like.

When muffins are done baking, cool them slightly on a rack, then brush muffins with apricot jam glaze, and sprinkle corn flakes on top, pressing lightly to adhere.

PER MUFFIN: 139 calories, 22 grams carbohydrate, 1 gram fat, 15 grams protein.

"Filling In" Fig Bars

MAKES 24 BARS

¾ cup shortening
2 eggs
1 cup white sugar
1 teaspoon vanilla extract
2 cups all-purpose flour
½ teaspoon baking soda
2 teaspoons baking powder
2 cups fig preserves

Fig Newtons and a glass of milk are a solid choice for pre-game snack. This homemade version is a bit healthier and has no additives.

Preheat oven to 375°F.

Cream together shortening, eggs, sugar, and vanilla. Sift flour, soda, and baking powder. Add to egg mixture.

Grease a small cookie sheet with shortening. Pour half of the dough into a pan and spread. Pour fig preserves over the dough and gently spread. Drop rest of dough over figs. Place in oven. When mixture starts to melt and gets soft, evenly spread the top. Bake for 40 minutes. Cool and cut into bars.

PER SERVING: 268 calories, 33 grams carbohydrate, 13.9 grams fat, 3.2 grams protein.

FILLING IN:

the player is temporarily covering a teammate's position.

"Soft Goal" Pretzels

SERVES 12

Canola or olive oil
   cooking spray
1⅓ cups warm water
1 package dry active yeast
1 tablespoon sugar
½ teaspoon kosher salt
   (or table salt)
3 cups all-purpose flour, divided
1 large egg
1 tablespoon cold water
2 tablespoons coarse salt

If you find yourself needing to knead, this is the homemade-dough version of the "Bend It" Baked Pretzels on page 130. Pretzels are a fun recipe to make with kids. They can twist theirs into shapes they invent. As a pre-game snack, serve with juice for optimal effect.

Place an oven rack in the center of an oven preheated to 425°F. Spray 2 baking sheets with the cooking oil.

Pour the warm water into a large mixing bowl, sprinkle yeast over the water, and let stand for about 5 minutes. Stir until completely dissolved. Add sugar, salt, and 1 cup of flour; stir until blended. Add 2 more cups of flour, ½ cup at a time, stirring to blend after each addition. The dough should be well blended.

Turn the dough onto a floured surface. Knead until the dough is smooth and elastic, sprinkling with flour if the dough is sticky. Pull the dough into 12 equal pieces. Roll 1 piece into a rope about 15 inches or any length you desire, depending on the size of the twisted creation you want to make. Twist into heart or desired shape. Put the pretzel on a baking sheet and continue with the remaining dough.

Beat the egg in a small bowl and add cold water. Beat together. Brush the egg wash over each pretzel using a pastry brush. Sprinkle the salt over the pretzels. Bake until golden brown, about 15–20 minutes. Cool on a baking rack before serving.

PER SERVING: 123 calories, 13 grams carbohydrate; 5 grams fat, 6 grams protein.

SOFT GOAL:

a goal given up by a goalkeeper on what should have been an easy save.

"Finisher" Ginger-Carrot Loaf

SERVES 8

Canola oil cooking spray
¾ cup sugar
⅓ cup canola oil
2 eggs
1 teaspoon vanilla extract
1 cup carrot juice
1½ cups all-purpose flour
¾ teaspoon ground ginger
2 teaspoons baking powder
½ teaspoon salt
½ cup pecans, toasted, chopped

This quick bread is easy to make, and one slice makes a lovely before-the-action snack. Slather a pat of cream cheese on top for an equally lovely breakfast treat.

Preheat oven to 350°F. Lightly spray a 1½-quart loaf pan with oil.

In a large bowl, whisk together sugar, oil, eggs, vanilla, and carrot juice.

In a medium bowl, mix flour, ginger, baking powder, and salt. Combine the flour and egg mixtures. Fold the pecans into the batter.

Pour into loaf pan; bake until toothpick inserted in center comes out clean, about 45–55 minutes. Transfer to wire rack; allow to cool in pan for 10 minutes, then invert loaf onto rack, and let cool further. Slice to serve.

NOTE: You can use 1 cup of carrot baby food in place of the 1 cup carrot juice.

PER SERVING: 321 calories, 41.5 grams carbohydrate, 15.4 grams fat, 5.4 grams protein.

FINISHER:

a striker who has the ability to "put away" or score on the opportunities given.

DURING-GAME SNACKS
"Quick Boost" Frosty Fruit Cups

SERVES 12

12 cupcake liners
6 medium, ripe bananas, diced
1 can (20 ounces) crushed
    pineapple, including juice
2 cans (15.25 ounces each)
    juice-packed apricot
    halves, undrained
2 tablespoons lemon juice
1 can (12 ounces) pineapple-
    peach-mango juice
12 ounces water

Keep these in an iced cooler for travel. Spoons are a must!

Place cupcake liners in one 12-count muffin tin. Combine all ingredients, mix well, and spoon into liners. Freeze. Place the frozen cups in freezer storage bags.

PER SERVING: 151 calories, 36 grams carbohydrate, .1 grams fat, 1.6 grams protein.

"Goalkeeper" Grape Water

SERVES 4

3 cups water
1 cup 100-percent grape juice,
    no added sugar

AN EASY ALTERNATIVE to expensive "flavored water." You can do this with other highly concentrated juices as well. Encourages fluid consumption for those that don't like plain water.

Combine and chill. Serve with crushed ice, if available. For quantity, mix 3 parts water to 1 part juice.

PER 1 CUP SERVING: 40 calories, 9.5 grams carbohydrate, 0.1 grams fat, 0.4 grams protein.

"Brain Freeze" Frozen Grapes and Berries

SERVES 6

2 cups green grapes
2 cups red grapes
2 cups blueberries

Cold but refreshing! No running while eating though!

Rinse fruit and dry on paper towels. Combine and place in a freezer storage bag. Lay in a single layer in freezer. Freeze overnight. For game day treat, store in ice chest with ice above and below bag. Take small cups for serving.

PER ½ CUP SERVING: 115 calories, 25.8 grams carbohydrate, .8 grams fat, 1 grams protein.

"Quick Pass" PB Roll-Ups

SERVES 4

For the child that missed breakfast, this will help the fueling efforts.

4 flour tortillas
4 tablespoons peanut butter
4 tablespoons apple butter
⅛ teaspoon cinnamon

Warm tortillas in microwave about 20 seconds. Spread each with 1 tablespoon peanut butter and 1 tablespoon apple butter. Lightly sprinkle total of ⅛ teaspoon cinnamon over all. Roll up and wrap individually in plastic wrap. Chill.

PER ROLL-UP: 292 calories, 36 grams carbohydrate, 13.2 grams fat, 7.2 grams protein.

"Fleet Feet" Baked Squash Seed

SERVES 4

1 cup winter squash seeds
1 tablespoon olive oil
½ teaspoon salt, or to taste

Roasted pumpkin seeds and dried fruit make a beautifully simple trail mix, with a balance of carb, fat, and protein. But did you know that you can also sub in seeds from butternut or acorn squash?

Preheat the oven to 275°F. Line a baking sheet with parchment paper or aluminum foil.

After removing the seeds from the squash, rinse with water, and remove any strings and bits of flesh. Pat dry and place in a small bowl. Toss the olive oil and salt with the seeds to evenly coat. Spread in an even layer on the prepared baking sheet.

Bake for 15 minutes or until seeds start to pop. Remove from oven and cool on the baking sheet before serving.

PER SERVING: 216 calories, 6.1 grams carbohydrate, 19.2 grams fat, 8.5 grams protein.

POST-GAME SNACKS

"Cracker" Snacker

SERVES 10

Canola or olive oil
　cooking spray
2 cups mini pretzels
2 cups Goldfish crackers
2 cups oyster crackers
2 cups Crispix cereal
2 cups Kix cereal
2 tablespoons canola
　margarine, melted
1 teaspoon Worcestershire sauce
½ teaspoon liquid smoke
¼ teaspoon garlic powder
1 tablespoon grated
　Parmesan cheese

This mix offers that much needed "post-game" carb load and adds some salt. Encourage water!

Preheat oven to 325°F. Spray 11-inch x 15-inch baking pan with nonstick cooking spray; set aside. Combine pretzels, crackers, and cereal in a large bowl; set aside. Combine the remaining ingredients, except the cheese, in a liquid measuring cup. Pour over the cracker-cereal mixture; lightly toss to cover. Add Parmesan cheese and toss. Pour onto the baking pan. Bake 20 minutes, stirring after 10 minutes.

PER CUP: 203 calories, 35.3 grams carbohydrate, 5.1 grams fat, 3.9 grams protein.

CRACKER:

(British slang for) a hard shot.

"Straight-Up" Fresh Strawberries and Cream

SERVES 6

3 pints strawberries,
   gently rinsed
8 ounces low-fat cream
   cheese, whipped
¾ cup Key lime low-fat yogurt
⅓ cup brown sugar
2 tablespoons low-fat milk
   (1 percent fat)
¼ teaspoon vanilla

Refreshing and full of vitamin C. The cream offers some extra carbs for refueling.

Drain strawberries, leaving stems on for dipping. Combine cream cheese and yogurt; blend well. Stir remaining ingredients in until brown sugar is dissolved. Serve strawberries whole with ¼ cup cream to dip.

PER SERVING (½ cup with 1 cup strawberries): 224 calories, 27.8 grams carbohydrate, 10 grams fat, 6.3 grams protein.

STRAIGHT-UP:

a run (play, movement) that is directly down the center of the field toward the goal.

"Bend It" Baked Pretzels

SERVES 24

1 package frozen dinner rolls
    (about 24), white or whole
    wheat, thawed
Canola or olive oil
    cooking spray
1 egg white, slightly beaten
    with 1 teaspoon water
Kosher salt

Of course these are best straight from the oven, but they're also a good, nonperishable power-boosting carb that kids will enjoy.

Thaw rolls, but prior to rising, roll them on a lightly floured cutting board into a rope about 12 inches long. On baking sheets sprayed with nonstick cooking spray, shape the rope into a pretzel, leaving at least 1 inch between pretzels. Let sit for 20 minutes, covered loosely with wax paper.

Preheat oven to 350°F about 10 minutes prior to baking pretzels. Prepare a shallow pan of boiling water to place on the lower oven rack while pretzels are baking.

Lightly brush egg white mixture on each pretzel and sprinkle with about ⅛ teaspoon salt just before baking. Bake 20 minutes or until golden brown.

NOTE: You may also use frozen breadstick dough, when available.

PER PRETZEL: 155 calories, 27 grams carbohydrate, 3 grams fat, 5.1 grams protein.

BEND IT:

to make the ball curve (around a "wall," or defensive line of players).

"Are You *Kidding?*" PB and Chocolate Bread

MAKES 1 LOAF

Canola oil cooking spray
1 cup flour
1 cup whole wheat flour
⅔ cup sugar
2 teaspoons baking powder
¼ teaspoon salt
1 cup peanut butter, smooth
　or crunchy
2 tablespoons canola oil
2 tablespoons egg substitute,
　such as Egg Beaters
1 cup low-fat milk
　(1 percent fat)
½ cup mini chocolate chips

Sounds unhealthy but . . . all things in moderation. At this point "in the game," kids need calories for refueling, and this bread contributes lots of carbs. The peanut butter also provides fat and protein to help satisfy hunger.

Preheat oven to 350°F. Spray the bottom of a 9-inch x 5-inch loaf pan with nonstick cooking spray.

In a medium bowl, combine flours, sugar, baking powder, and salt; set aside.

Blend together the peanut butter, oil, and egg substitute; stir in milk and mix well. Add liquid ingredients to dry ingredients and stir until well blended. Fold in chocolate chips. Spoon batter into prepared pan. Bake 45–50 minutes or until golden brown and a toothpick inserted in middle comes out clean. Let cool in pan 10–15 minutes. Remove and place on cooling rack. Store in fridge.

PER SLICE: 388 calories, 44 grams carbohydrate, 19 grams fat, 10.5 grams protein.

"Trail Pass" Trail Mix

SERVES 9

2 cups Golden Grahams cereal
1 cup dried pineapple
½ cup dried cranberries
½ cup raisins
¾ cup toasted pecan halves

Another balanced mix of carbohydrate, fat, and protein. Dried fruits are more dense in calories than fresh, but again, what better time to have this "high octane" source of fuel?

Combine all ingredients. Pour into Ziploc bag.

PER ½ CUP SERVING: 230 calories, 29.4 grams carbohydrate, 11.3 grams fat, 2.5 grams protein.

TRAILING PASS:

a backwards pass.

"Home Team" Hummus

SERVES 6

1 can (16 ounces) garbanzo
    beans, drained, rinsed
1 stalk celery, finely diced
¼ cup parsley, finely diced
1 clove garlic, minced
1 teaspoon ground cumin
¼ teaspoon cayenne
1 tomato, finely diced

This classic Mediterranean dip is delicious on toasted pita wedges or chips, but it's also an easy and super-nutritious spread for sandwiches and wraps.

Blend together all ingredients except tomatoes in a food processor or blender until smooth. Add tomatoes and stir until blended.

PER SERVING: 282 calories, 47 grams carbohydrate, 4 grams fat, 15 grams protein.

"Scoop It" Strawberry Oatmeal

SERVES 4

1 pint strawberries, hulled,
   thinly sliced
1–2 tablespoons brown sugar,
   firmly packed
1¾ cups warm water
1¾ cups low-fat milk
   (1 percent fat)
¼ teaspoon salt
2 cups quick-cooking oats
½ cup plain low-fat yogurt
Brown sugar for
   sprinkling, optional

Breakfast cereal is a great snack any time. Why not sub in this healthy and filling home-cooked version?

Toss the strawberries and brown sugar together and let sit for 5 minutes and reserve for later use.

Combine water, milk, and salt in a medium saucepan over medium heat. Fold in oats and cook, stirring occasionally, until thickened, about 5–6 minutes.

Scoop oatmeal into 4 bowls, top each serving with a dollop of yogurt, ½ cup of the reserved strawberries and brown sugar mixure, and sprinkle tops with additional brown sugar.

PER SERVING: 267 calories, 46.3 grams carbohydrate, 5.4 grams fat, 11.6 grams protein.

SCOOP (Ball; Pass, etc.):

A short-distance pass that is predominately vertical in nature, achieved more by lifting the ball with the foot than striking the ball.

"Parry" Pineapple Parfait

SERVES 1

¼ cup cottage cheese
2 teaspoons honey
¾ cup diced pineapple
Shredded sweetened toasted
   coconut, optional

Like the "Free Kick" Fruity Yogurt Parfait (page 49), this parfait is great as a snack, breakfast, or dessert. Plus, it's a great source of carbs, protein, and fiber.

With a hand blender, whip together the cottage cheese and honey.

In a large glass, layer a third of the pineapple and half the whipped cottage cheese-honey mixture. Repeat layer. Top with remaining third of the pineapple, then garnish with shredded coconut.

PER SERVING: 232 calories, 41 grams carbohydrate, 1.1 grams fat, 16.7 grams protein.

PARRY:

(v) to knock or push the ball away in a controlled or directed manner; *(n)* a controlled redirection of the ball by the goalkeeper.

"Center Circle" Grape and Cream Cheese Pizza

SERVES 1

Butter
2 tablespoons cream cheese
1 whole wheat tortilla
½ cup red seedless grapes,
   sliced in half lengthwise
1 teaspoon sugar
½ teaspoon cinnamon

These "pizzas" are a great refueling option, and kids can create their own designs and patterns with the grapes.

Preheat oven to 375°F. Lightly coat a baking sheet with butter.

Spread cream cheese on tortilla; arrange grapes, cut side up, in the cream cheese, pressing gently.

Mix together sugar and cinnamon and sprinkle over cream cheese pizza.

Bake until crisp, about 15–18 minutes.

Some other options:
- Try using cheddar cheese spread and pear slices.
- In place of grapes, arrange craisins (cranberry-flavored raisins) and walnuts in the cream cheese.
- Use a fruit-flavored cream cheese, and top with your favorite dried fruit and nuts.
- Opt for a savory- or sweet-flavored cream cheese, such as veggie or garlic and add sliced cucumber—or strawberry or berry topped with your favorite fresh fruits.

PER SERVING: 291 calories, 37.2 grams carbohydrate, 14.2 grams fat, 5.5 grams protein.

CENTER CIRCLE:

a circular marking with a 10-yard radius in the center of the field where kickoffs are held (in center) to start or restart the game.

"On the Ball" Oven Fries

SERVES 2

Olive oil spray
1 large egg white
2 teaspoons spice (e.g., chili powder, lemon pepper, thyme, Mrs. Dash)
2 medium baking potatoes, sliced into wedges or French-cut
2 tablespoons ketchup

French fries are pretty much everyone's favorite snack. These "fries," however, aren't fried at all. They're baked in the oven, so less fat and less grease in the kitchen.

Preheat oven to 450°F. Spray baking sheet with olive oil.

Combine egg white and spices and coat potato pieces with the mixture. You can use a large Ziploc bag to do this or gently toss together as with a salad.

Place spice-coated potatoes on the baking sheet in a single layer, with space between each. Put in oven and reduce heat to 400°F. Bake "fries" for 35–45 minutes, turning them occasionally to brown evenly. Serve hot with ketchup.

PER SERVING: 140 calories, 26 grams carbohydrate, 1 gram fat, 4 grams protein.

ON THE BALL:

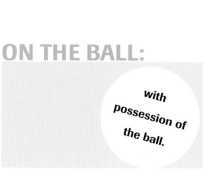

with possession of the ball.

"Stick It" Veggie Kebabs

SERVES 4

8 bamboo skewers
   (9 inches long)
1 celery stalk, cut in
   1-inch pieces
1 package cherry tomatoes
1 small zucchini, cut in
   1-inch pieces
1 small head broccoli, cut into
   florets (pre-steamed for
   3 minutes for best texture)
1 medium green or red bell
   pepper, cut into cubes

It's a weird phenomenon, but kids love food on sticks. These skewered veggies make a fun and super-healthy after-game snack to replenish energy stores.

On each skewer, spear 1 piece of celery, tomato, zucchini, broccoli, and bell pepper. Serve with "Creative Play" Artichoke Dip (page 139).

PER SERVING (with "Creative Play" Artichoke Dip): 139 calories, 22 grams carbohydrate, 1 gram fat, 15 grams protein.

STICK:

to go for the tackle.

"Creative Play" Artichoke Dip

MAKES ABOUT 2 CUPS

1 cup canned artichokes packed
   in water, drained
½ teaspoon onion powder
1 cup low-fat cottage cheese
2–3 tablespoons skim milk
2 green onions, diced

This dip is a mouth-wateringly good way to get kids to munch on raw veggies—on or off a stick. It's nice with baked chips or pretzels, too.

Put ingredients into food processor or blender, and blend till smooth. Refrigerate for 30 minutes or more before serving.

CREATIVE PLAY:

a play that many players and spectators would not have thought of.

"Rookies" Pumpkin Oatmeal Cookies

MAKES 2 DOZEN

1 cup all-purpose flour
½ cup quick-cooking oats
½ teaspoon baking soda
½ teaspoon ground cinnamon
¼ teaspoon salt
½ cup butter, softened
½ cup brown sugar
½ cup white sugar
1 egg
½ teaspoon vanilla extract
½ cup canned pumpkin puree
1 cup raisins

These cookies are a sweet treat, but pumpkin provides an added shot of vitamins A and C, potassium, dietary fiber, and manganese.

Preheat oven to 350°F. Combine the flour, oats, baking soda, cinnamon, and salt; set aside.

In a large bowl, cream together until smooth the butter, brown sugar, and white sugar. Beat in the egg and vanilla, then stir in the pumpkin puree. Stir in the dry ingredients until well blended. Mix in raisins. Drop by rounded spoonfuls onto ungreased cookie sheets.

Bake for 8–10 minutes. Allow cookies to cool on a baking sheet for 5 minutes before removing to a wire cooling rack.

NOTE: You can up the carbs and lower the fat by using ⅓ cup butter and ⅔ cup pumpkin puree, rather than ½ cup of each.

PER COOKIE: 105 calories, 16.1 grams carbohydrate, 4.2 grams fat, 1.3 grams protein.

"Round Robin" Apple O's

SERVES 1

1 apple, cored, sliced crosswise
   into 3 thick rings
3 tablespoons peanut butter
   or other nut butter
1 tablespoon granola
1 tablespoon toasted coconut
1 tablespoon cereal, such as
   puffed rice
1 tablespoon dried apricots,
   chopped

With rings of apple as
foundation, these healthy snacks
work with just about any topping
you sprinkle on them.

Spread 1 side of each apple ring
with 1 tablespoon peanut butter.

Top each apple ring with a blend of
the remaining ingredients, or with
"Trail Pass" Trail Mix (page 132).

PER SERVING: 243 calories,
31.9 grams carbohydrate,
12 grams fat, 6.3 grams protein.

"Deflection" Deviled Eggs

SERVES 8

4 whole eggs in the shell,
  hardboiled
2 avocados, peeled, pitted,
  mashed
1 tablespoon chopped cilantro
1 tablespoon minced
  green onion
2 teaspoons seeded,
  minced jalapeño
2 teaspoons fresh lime juice
½ teaspoon salt, or to taste
1 dash hot pepper sauce (such
  as Tabasco), or to taste
1 teaspoon Worcestershire sauce,
  or to taste
1 teaspoon Dijon-style
  prepared mustard
1 pinch paprika

These are yum-yummy deviled eggs of a different color—guacamole green. They're not particularly loaded with carbs, so you'll want to serve them with veggies and/or sparkling juice.

Peel and slice eggs in half; remove yolks to a mixing bowl.

In the bowl with the yolks, combine the avocado, cilantro, green onion, and jalapeño. Stir in the lime juice, and season with salt, hot sauce, Worcestershire, and mustard.

Feel free to skip any seasoning ingredient. Let your family's tastes be your guide. Mix well; and fill empty egg white halves. Chill.

Sprinkle with paprika just before serving.

PER SERVING: 121 calories, 4.5 grams carbohydrate, 10.3 grams fat, 4.2 grams protein.

DEFLECTION: the ricochet of a ball after it hits a player (including the goalkeeper) or a referee.

"Recovery Run" Zuccocoa Muffins

MAKES 24

Cooking spray for greasing
3 eggs
1 cup brown sugar
1 cup white sugar
½ cup canola oil
½ cup applesauce
⅓ cup unsweetened
   cocoa powder
1½ teaspoons vanilla extract
2 cups grated zucchini
3 cups all-purpose flour
1 teaspoon baking soda
½ teaspoon baking powder
1 teaspoon salt
1¼ teaspoons pumpkin pie spice

These zucchini muffins with a touch of cocoa may seem like an over-indulgence, but they're a great tank refueler, with the right amount of carbs and a bit of fiber, too.

Preheat oven to 350°F. Lightly grease two 12-cup muffin tins or line with paper liners.

In a large bowl, beat the eggs; then beat in the sugars, oil, and applesauce. Add the cocoa, vanilla, and zucchini and stir well.

Stir in the flour, baking soda, baking powder, salt, and pumpkin pie spice. Mix until just moist.

Pour batter into prepared muffin tins filling two-thirds of the way full. Bake at 350°F for 20–25 minutes. Remove from pan and let cool on a wire rack. Store loosely covered.

PER MUFFIN: 176 calories, 29.7 grams carbohydrate, 5.2 grams fat, 2.7 grams protein.

RECOVERY RUN:

a run made backward to get behind the ball after being beaten.

"Engine Room" English Muffin
With Fruit & Melted Cheese

SERVES 1

½ apple, thinly sliced
1 wholegrain English muffin or
   bagel, split, lightly toasted
⅓ cup grated cheddar cheese

There's no doubt this nutritious and substantial nibble will satisfy after a workout.

Place apple slices in equal portions onto the cut side of toasted muffin or bagel halves. Sprinkle grated cheese in equal portions over the apples.

In the toaster oven or on a baking sheet under the broiler, broil muffins until cheese is melted. Serve warm.

Some other options:
- Toasted oat-bran English muffin with peanut butter and grapes.
- Pear slices and Gouda as toppings for muffin or bagel.
- Pineapple chunks, cashews, and mozzarella as toppings for muffin or bagel.
- Dill pickle slices and cheddar (an acquired taste, perhaps, but really, it's just a patty-less cheeseburger) as toppings for muffin or bagel.

PER SERVING: 346 calories, 37.3 grams carbohydrate, 15.4 grams fat, 15.1 grams protein.

 # Timely Tips for Quick-to-Fix Food

My best tip for busy families? Take time to plan. Sit down prior to the beginning of each week for a family meeting. This allows not only for planning, but for great communication as well. With a calendar or "Blank Menu Chart" (see page 149), like the example shown, you can note the week's activities and also document menu items. Don't get bogged in minute details. You don't have to have menus for three meals per day for seven days chiseled in stone. Timesaving is the goal . . . not more work. First, identify tightly scheduled days, then make realistic plans with one of the following options:

- Leftovers
- Eating out
- Prep early morning or the preceding night with a slow cooker item
- Make it "build a sub" night and have the necessary ingredients on hand

Any of these ideas are better than finally getting home at 8 p.m. or after, with everyone hungry and no plans to accommodate.

When planning a menu, get input from others on what they'd like and how they can assist. Include the weekly grocery ad (as well as coupons . . . great for kids to clip!) in planning to take advantage of sale items. Take special care to look for items, normally higher-priced, that might be an option to include, especially if coupons are available. Some of the produce and deli items appear too expensive at face value, but consider the following: in buying produce, you're most likely paying by the pound for some waste as well. It doesn't do much good to buy a variety of fruits and veggies if there is no time to prep them and they end up spoiling. This is where some of the prepackaged veggies, salads, and fruits make sense. These items also lend more variety. The wide array of prepackaged salads contain a variety of veggies, and you can combine them to add even more variety. You could add fresh spinach, for example. In any case, be sure to make quality a top concern, as some prepackaged fruits tend to lose some quality.

When grocery-shopping, always take a list, loosely organized according to the store's floor plan, if possible, and never go when you're hungry. Take care when buying meat products to remember that "waste" is part of the price per pound, just as it is with produce. Leaner meats (especially ground) mean less loss in cooking, just as boneless, skinless chicken may actually be less expensive when considering the cost of the bone, skin, and prep time. Again, when planning, the grocery ad and personal preferences dictate menus.

Sometimes it makes sense to have frozen or convenience items on hand. Remember that you don't have to literally follow the package instructions when it comes to prep. You can often cut added fat in half without sacrificing quality. The addition of appropriate supplemental ingredients such as rice, pasta, or veggies increases volume, decreases calories per serving (possibly fat and sodium, too), and "freshens" the food item.

Use food items such as meal replacement or energy drinks and bars in moderation. Scrutinize the actual ingredient and nutrient contributions as compared to daily intake recommendations. Cost is most likely high; make sure it isn't just for a "glorified" candy bar or sweet drink. Most importantly . . . discriminate taste!! If the review is no better than, "These don't taste so bad," why include them at all? Again, planning ahead minimizes the need for these types of products.

To wrap it all up, we live in a fast-paced world that makes instant gratification oh-so tempting. We want what we want when we want it, and we don't want to suffer any consequences. Unfortunately, that is more the mindset of a two-year-old.

In striving to combine healthful eating and daily exercise, you are following the most worthwhile prescription for quality, healthy living for ourselves, and for the future . . . our children.

"The great end of life is not knowledge but action." (*Thomas Henry Huxley*)

So . . . get in the game!!

Blank Menu Chart

	BREAKFAST	LUNCH	DINNER	SNACK
Sunday				
Monday				
Tuesday				
Wednesday				
Thursday				
Friday				
Saturday				

GROCERIES TO BUY	QUANTITY	✓	GROCERIES TO BUY	QUANTITY	✓

Index